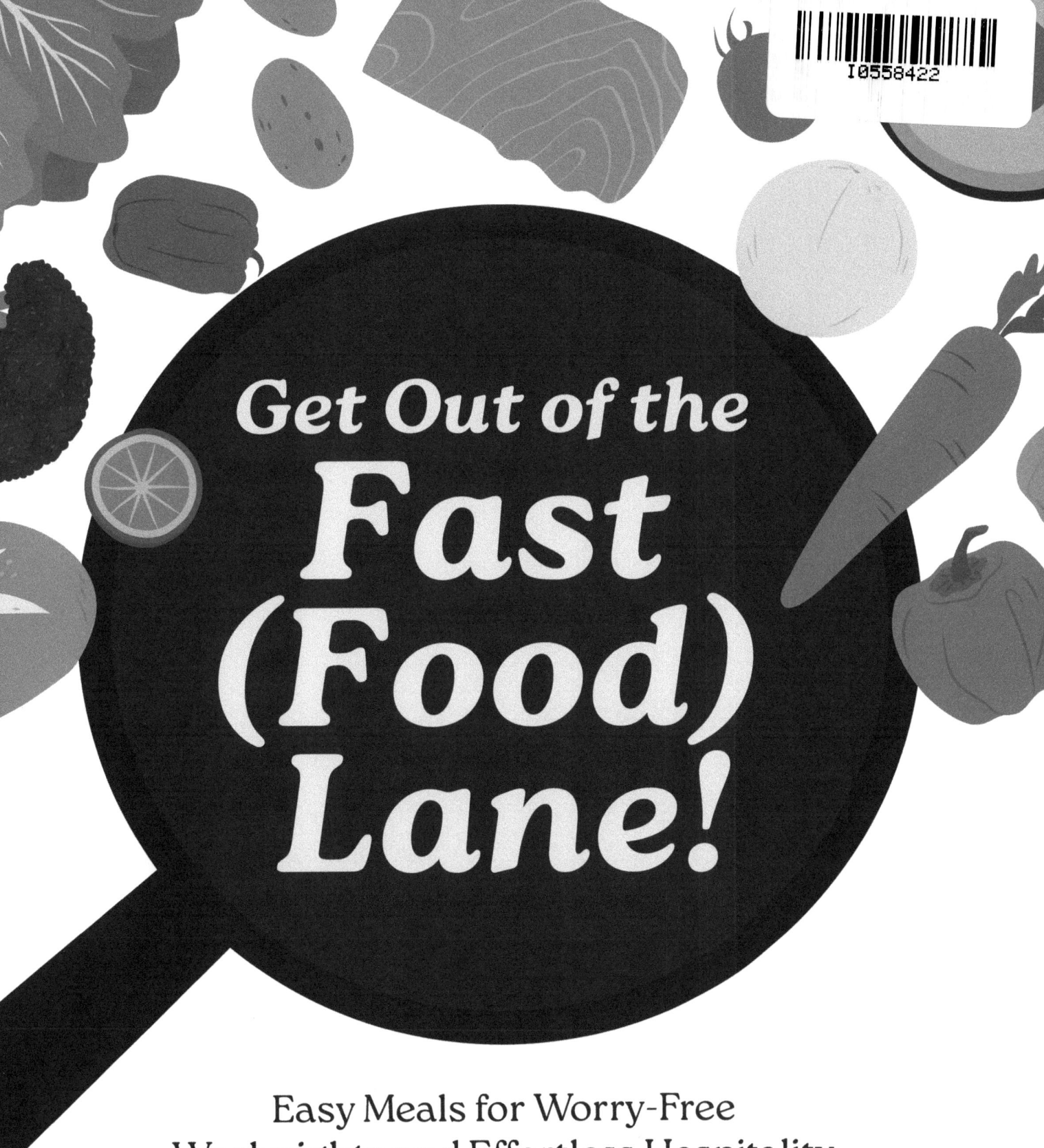

Get Out of the Fast (Food) Lane!

Easy Meals for Worry-Free Weeknights and Effortless Hospitality

TONI R. YOUNG-HUBER

Get Out of the Fast (Food) Lane!

Easy Meals for Worry-Free Weeknights
and Effortless Hospitality

Toni R. Young-Huber

2024© by Toni R. Young-Huber

All rights reserved. Published 2024.

BIBLE SCRIPTURES

Printed in the United States of America
Spirit Media and our logos are trademarks of Spirit Media

SpiritMedia.US

www.spiritmedia.us
8045 Arco Corporate Dr STE 130
Raleigh, NC 27617
1 (888) 800-3744

Books>Cookbooks, Food & Wine>Cooking Methods>Quick & Easy

Paperback ISBN: 979-8-89307-030-9
Hardback ISBN: 979-8-89307-031-6
eBook ISBN: 979-8-89307-029-3
Library of Congress Control Number: 2024903664

TABLE OF CONTENTS

Author's Introduction

This cookbook grew out of the many Sunday afternoons I spent teaching a coworker from India how to cook American foods. We were both working as traveling nurses in North Carolina. Terrence was looking for a way to break the fast-food habit and feed himself. Once he discovered Southern foods, we were off to the races! I let him know: If he would tell me what he wanted to make, we would make it together. He'd do all the work, but I would help him succeed. And succeed he did!

I grew up on a farm watching my grandmother cook three big meals a day. In my culture, women feed their families. It's a point of pride and a love language. So cooking for and with other people comes naturally to me. For me, cooking can be therapeutic. The process of preparing produce, chopping and slicing, stirring, sauteing and frying, requires thoughtfulness and attention to detail.

All these preparations are simple and have only a few steps. Some recipes are entirely from scratch while others will take a prepared food and enhance it with a few substitutions. The ingredients are inexpensive and easy to buy. Feel free to experiment and put your own spin on any of the dishes in this book.

One key to learning how to cook is to not be too hard on yourself. Give yourself grace when you make mistakes. What you serve doesn't have to be pretty to taste good, though we all want to serve dishes that are pleasing to the eye. Just begin slowly, and learn a few terms and techniques and grow as you go.

I've cooked all these recipes so many times that I'm quite confident in them. Still, the first time you cook something is a bit of an experiment. You may be more confident if you've done something similar in the past, but you're never certain how you'll like the flavors, textures, and more, the first time you cook a dish. If it comes out well, you can refine the technique and the ingredients next time.

When we share food we offer friendship, hospitality, and love. Every culture uses food to show love. Each generation nurtures and nourishes the next. So whether you're a seasoned cook or a beginner, these recipes are for you! Whether you are in the kitchen alone or with family and friends, settle in for a life journey and enjoy the ride! You can feed yourself tonight and sustain yourself until tomorrow. Your sense of adventure can start in your kitchen.

Be encouraged. Start today and never give up!

But I've Always Been a Kitchen Failure!

Let's start by defining "failure." What if your dish doesn't look like the one in Taste of Home? Did you fail? No way! What you don't know is how they got the glorious shine on that roast turkey. They didn't cook it to perfection. They shellacked that bird for the photo shoot!

Perfection is elusive and appearances are just that—appearances. Your dish will never look like the one in the pictures and it will always taste better. You don't have to throw a dish away because it's ugly. Not every tomato is worthy of a picture on the cover of a magazine, but every tomato adds flavor to tomato sauce. Sometimes the best thing you can do is serve something that looks like crap and tastes delicious.

You probably didn't snow ski the first time up. Cooking is the same. Cooking is a process with a learning curve. Give yourself grace! There are lots of really simple recipes here that you can do from the start. Check out Five-Ingredient Chicken Pot Pie in the Main Dish Casseroles section to learn how a friend who never cooked at all made a dinner she couldn't believe from this recipe.

The great thing about cooking is that you're doing it to please yourself. If you make it and you don't like it, you never have to cook it again. If you like it, you'll try again, and maybe change it up a bit so you like it even more.

But I Don't Have Time to Cook!

People are busy today, and I'm always hearing them say, "I'm too busy to cook," or "I don't have time to cook."

I want to challenge you to rethink that idea.

Do you have time to wait for someone to deliver your meal? To sit in a long line at the drive through? Do you have money you just urgently need to empty out of your pocket to pay for a restaurant meal? With a quick trip to the grocery store, you could be home enjoying family time with people you care about while you cook a meal for them. And when you serve that home-cooked meal, you know exactly what's in it.

Where do you want to spend that thirty minutes? Waiting in a drive through or walking through the produce section choosing the onions and potatoes you're going to make into a meal? Do you want to spend forty dollars on a steak dinner in a restaurant or ten dollars on a steak that you perfect yourself?

If it's a busy night, you don't have to make a meatloaf that takes an hour to bake. You can make buttered noodles with parmesan cheese and that's dinner. If you've taken the time to prepare a main dish, you can buy the sides ready-made. Ina Garten, the "Barefoot Contessa," buys Bob Evans mashed potatoes from the supermarket and just puts them in a bowl and serves them! (Okay, she does mix in some sour cream and parmesan cheese, but how much work is that?)

You don't have to produce everything on the table to be a successful cook. You don't have to prepare every part of the meal for it to be a really good, successful meal. When Terrance learned to make a delicious baked-salmon main course, I told him: Go buy some frozen peas and Uncle Ben's ninety-second rice, and that's your dinner!

The process of preparing and eating a meal takes the same amount of time whether you cook it yourself, wait in a drive through, or go out to eat. The decision you have to make is where you want to invest your time and money. If you're telling me you don't have time to cook, I'm thinking you're intimidated. That's why I wrote this book—to let you know how easy it can be to make meals for yourself, your family, and your friends.

So choose just one dish you want to master and fill everything else in with store-bought sides. You'll have the satisfaction of learning a new skill and you'll be eating better than you will ever imagine.

Creating Your Own Recipe Variations

Cookbooks written in other times often encourage the home cook to vary the recipes. That approach allowed for creativity, and it also allowed for the fact that provisions weren't always guaranteed. During World War II, for instance, you might not have seen ham for several years, but you were likely to have cans of Spam. During COVID-19, local supermarkets were short of lots of basic foods for weeks. Desperation breeds inventiveness, and many discovered what they could substitute successfully for many recipe ingredients.

I encourage people to test their ideas by scooping a single portion into a bowl and testing their variation on that portion. That way you don't have to risk a whole dish to try a new idea. See what happens when you add sour cream. . .mix in some parsley or cilantro. . .use a different cheese. You'll discover new ways to prepare your favorites so they are just right for you. When you discover combinations that you like, you can try those flavors together in a different dish. Likewise, if a recipe has an ingredient that you really dislike, substitute by using another similar ingredient. You can ruin my day by putting blue cheese crumbles on a salad! So just put a different cheese on.

Baked goods are more finicky, so there are fewer variations you can safely try before you've built up some skill. At the beginning, I would encourage you to limit baking experiments to trying a different flavoring extract or adding some fruit zest to the dough or batter. If there is an icing or topping, you can change that up without risking the rise and the bake.

You'll find some suggested variations from many of my recipes. I'll have succeeded as your cooking teacher when you can say, "I made that recipe, but it wasn't exactly like yours. This is how I changed it, and it came out just as good. . .maybe better!"

Creating your own version of a dish can become the most fun part of cooking. I can't wait to hear how much you are enjoying it!

Feed People with Love

Finally, remember: When you go to cook, you're speaking a love language. I can't say that too strongly. Jesus cooked fish on a fire to feed his followers. Jesus shared bread and fish to feed thousands of people who had come to hear him speak. When you're feeding anyone—whether yourself or someone else—you're showing your love. Say a prayer for success and trust God to help you succeed, because God cares to feed all the people He loves.

Main Dishes

When my late husband and I lived in Colorado, we enjoyed a constant flow of weekend guests. People would come on Friday after work and stay until Sunday afternoon. We lived in the foothills above Denver, up in the mountains where there was no traffic, no city bustle, making it a great respite for people. Friday night, we'd just sit on the porch and put something in the smoker or on the grill for dinner. We'd figure out together what we wanted to eat for the rest of the weekend. Saturday morning, we'd go out and get whatever we needed, then come back and cook. There was no agenda and no real plan for the weekend. The kids would be outside playing frisbee or ball, others might go out for a hike. You were in the mountains for the weekend and you could just relax, enjoy, and maybe do some cooking.

We had a lot of weeknight guests, too! Our house was kind of a kid-magnet. Our kids would always have other kids over because the other parents didn't cook like I did. Coming from my background, I always felt a sense of obligation to put a hot meal on the table every night. But it was not unusual for me to plan for four and end up serving eight or more! You just have to learn to stretch it. I've added tips for stretching meals in the section of Helpful Tips at the end of the book. When you cook some of these delicious but unfussy main dishes, you'll find your dinner table is in demand, too.

Chicken and Dumplings

This is a classic and simple stew that is perfect for cold fall days! I like to make it from scratch, but you could shortcut it by buying a rotisserie chicken and shredding it. In this instance, you will need canned chicken stock for the broth. When I taught my friend Cathy Vau how to make it, the part she found hardest was recognizing when the noodle dough was the right texture. It needs to be a bit wetter and tougher than pie crust, and stretchy enough that you can roll it as thin as you want. Once you've felt it, you'll never forget how to make this dough perfectly.

1 whole chicken (2-3 lbs.)

Water, to cover

2 tbsp. Better than Bouillon, chicken-flavored

2 tsp. salt

1 tsp. pepper

1 c. warm broth

4 eggs

All-Purpose Flour

In a large pot, cover the chicken with water and season with salt, pepper, and bouillon. Over medium heat, simmer gently until the juices run clear when pierced. Test by sticking a fork in the thickest part of the thigh to see that the juices run clear. Remove chicken from the pot and cool. When cool enough to handle, remove the meat from the bones and set aside. Take one cup of the cooking broth and set aside. Allow it to cool until tepid. While the broth is cooling, scramble four eggs in a large bowl. Then temper the eggs by adding small amounts of broth while stirring briskly. Add one teaspoon of salt and half a teaspoon of pepper. Add flour a cup at a time, stirring until you have a sticky dough.

Divide the dough into two, and on a floured surface, knead, adding flour until the dough is no longer sticky. Roll out to one fourth-inch thickness and cut into strips. Bring the remaining broth to a rolling boil and place the strips on top of the surface. They will sink but then will rise to the top. Cook, stirring occasionally, for twenty minutes, and then add chicken pieces back to the pot. Serve immediately. Enjoy!

Time-saving Tip: Now that I live alone, I don't make this dish in full quantity here. You can easily reduce the amounts of the ingredients, but here's my time-saving tip on how to handle the chicken. I still cook the 2-3 lb. chicken, but after the chicken has cooled and I've shredded it. I set most of the chicken meat aside for other dishes. You can put a third of the chicken meat into this dish, then use another third for chicken salad, and the rest for a simple soup (like the Chicken Noodle Soup in the Soups and Stews section). If you want, you can just pack up the shredded meat that doesn't go into tonight's chicken and dumplings and either use it in the same week or freeze it.

Cooking for One Tip: If you live alone and want to make a full pot, your coworkers will love you. Mine fall on this dish like wolves!

Baked Salmon

My student cook was amazed at how easy it is to make baked salmon! Sumac is a popular seasoning in Middle Eastern cooking. It is made from the berries of sumac trees. These berries are dark red and can be found either whole or in powdered form. Sumac's taste is very similar to lemon and it can be used as a lemon substitute sprinkled over finished dishes. The only reason I know about it is because we had a sumac tree in our yard as kids and we would suck on the berries. They were super sour! Some kinds of sumac are poisonous, so it's better to buy this ingredient than collect it on your own.

One 4-oz. salmon filet per person

Salt

Pepper

Powdered sumac

Panko breadcrumbs

Olive oil

Lemon wedges for serving

Preheat the oven to 400 degrees Fahrenheit.

Spray a cookie sheet or low pan with nonstick vegetable spray. Place filets skin-side down in the pan. Sprinkle sumac, salt and pepper over each filet. Cover the flesh side with breadcrumbs and moisten with olive oil. Place in oven and cook for twenty minutes, testing for doneness after that time. When done, the fish should flake easily with a fork.

Baked Chicken with Gravy

1 large chicken (4-6 lbs.)

Salt

Pepper

¼ c. melted butter

One whole lemon, halved

One head of garlic, cut crosswise

20 sprigs of thyme (3 tbsp. plus 1 tsp. dried)

4 carrots, quartered

6 new potatoes, cut in half

1 medium yellow onion, quartered

Preheat the oven to 425 degrees. Rinse the chicken inside and out and season with salt and pepper, making sure to salt and pepper the outside, and the cavity as well. Stuff the cavity with both halves of the lemon, the garlic, and the thyme. Season the vegetables with salt, pepper, and olive oil, and place them at the bottom of the pan. Place chicken on top of the vegetables and place it in the oven. Bake for one and a half hours hours until the juices run clear when pierced in the thickest part of the thigh. Remove from the oven and cover with a foil tent for twenty minutes.

Gravy

By reserving the pan juices from your roasted chicken, you can make gravy.

½ c. reserved pan juices

½ c. flour

2-3 c. chicken stock

Carefully scrape the baking dish, making sure to get all the brown bits. Transfer the pan juices to a skillet over medium heat. Sprinkle the flour evenly over the surface and cook for three to four minutes stirring constantly. This makes a roux. Constant stirring is key! It ensures that your gravy is not lumpy. After the flour has browned, pour in the chicken stock, bring to a boil, and then lower the heat and cook gently to make a smooth consistency. Serve over chicken and vegetables.

Variations: You can switch this recipe up by changing the vegetables used in the pan or by prepping the chicken differently. One suggestion is to slice the lemon very thinly and slide underneath the skin of the chicken, alternating with cloves of garlic.

Green Chili

I learned how to make this very versatile dish from my best friend in Denver, Cathy Vau. You can serve it as you would a traditional chili, in a bowl, with tortillas on the side. It is also delicious spooned over burritos or layered in a dish with tortillas and baked. A third suggestion is to serve it over two medium-cooked eggs with tortillas on the side—I think that's the very best way to have it! That's what huevos rancheros is—eggs with chili. I love the way green chili can serve as a soup or a sauce.

1 lb. ground pork

3 tbsp. olive oil

1½ tsp. salt

1 tsp. pepper

½ tsp. chipotle powder

½ tsp. red pepper flakes

1 tsp. cumin

1 medium yellow onion, diced

One 4 oz. can diced green chilis (hot or mild, depending on taste)

One 14.5 oz. can fire-roasted tomatoes, diced

One 10 oz. can Ro-Tel tomatoes (again, hot or mild)

2 c. chicken stock

2 c. grated Colby-Jack cheese

Brown pork in oil in a heavy-bottomed saucepan until crumbly. Add salt, pepper, Chipotle powder, red pepper flakes, and cumin, stirring to combine. Add onion and cook until translucent. Add green chilies, and sprinkle the flour over the surface, covering all. Cook, stirring, for three minutes to brown the flour slightly. Stir in diced tomatoes and Ro-Tel tomatoes. Add chicken stock and simmer for thirty minutes. Stir in grated cheese.

Chili

1 lb. ground beef

1½ tsp. salt

1 tsp. pepper

1 tsp. chipotle powder

1 tsp. red chili flakes

1 tsp. cumin

1 medium yellow onion, diced

One 4 oz. can diced green chilis

One 10 oz. can Ro-Tel tomatoes (heat level to your taste)

One 14.5 oz. can diced fire-roasted tomatoes

2 c. chicken stock or beef

One 15.5 oz. can red beans

One 15 oz. can black beans

Brown ground beef until crumbly and uniformly brown. Drain off any unwanted fat. Add salt, pepper, chipotle powder, chili flakes, and cumin. Add onion, and cook until translucent. Add Ro-Tel tomatoes and fire-roasted tomatoes. Stir until combined. Add chicken stock and the beans and simmer for thirty minutes. Serve in bowls while still hot, with tortillas or cornbread on the side.

Toppings: Some toppings for this chili include cheddar cheese, sour cream, jalapenos and oyster crackers.

Chicken Piccata

"Direct your children onto the right path, and when they are older, they will not leave it." (Prov. 22:6 NLT)

I never had a time when there were no kids who wanted to be in the kitchen with me. They'd put down the video games right away to come and cook. When my godson was in fifth grade, he'd hit the kitchen every afternoon, and all he wanted to do was pound chicken flat enough to grill. He learned some skills that have stood him in good stead as he's grown older.

I also remember when my son was in the fourth grade. He was such a perfectionist that he wouldn't try anything if he didn't think he'd get it right the first time. I think that's the problem for a lot of people in the kitchen. They don't want to waste their money, their time, their heart on something that doesn't succeed.

But kitchen success looks different at different times of life and even from one family member to another. I remember an entire year when my daughter was in high school and the only thing she ate was Lipton broccoli and rice casserole. She would make it from the package, microwave it, eat for two or three days, then make another one and start all over. My son, on the other hand, was a total garbage truck. You could give him your most failed meal and he'd say, "Mom, that was great, thanks!"

So don't let anyone's food fussiness stop you from feeling successful in the kitchen. And never forget that when you've helped your children make a habit of cooking—even if it's just reconstituting a commercial food product—you've directed them toward a way of life where they can nourish themselves and others.

This recipe requires you to pound the chicken thin, the same way my godson liked to do. A meat mallet is a great tool for this. Many people like to put plastic wrap on top of the meat before they pound it.

2 boneless, skinless chicken breasts sliced in half

salt

freshly ground black pepper

1 c. flour for dredging

2 large eggs, beaten

1 c. panko bread crumbs

6 tbsp. unsalted butter

5 tbsp. extra virgin olive oil, divided

⅓ c. fresh lemon juice

½ c. chicken stock

¼ c. capers, rinsed

⅓ fresh parsley, chopped, for garnish

Cooked angel hair or thin spaghetti pasta

Pound chicken to one fourth-inch thickness. Season with salt and pepper. Dredge the chicken first in flour, then the beaten eggs (letting the extra drip off), then the panko breadcrumbs. In a large skillet over medium-high heat, melt two tablespoons of butter and add two tablespoons of olive oil. When the butter has melted and starts to sizzle, place two pieces of the chicken into the skillet and cook for three minutes until browned. Turn it over and cook for another three minutes to brown. Transfer to a plate. Add two tablespoons of butter and two tablespoons of olive oil to pan, and when it starts to sizzle, cook the other chicken pieces. Remove to a plate. Into the pan, pour the lemon juice, chicken stock, and capers. Scrape up all the little brown bits in the pan as it deglazes. Check for seasoning and return chicken to the pan for five minutes. Remove the chicken to a platter. Add the last two tablespoons of butter and whisk vigorously. Pour sauce over the chicken and garnish with parsley. Serve over a bed of pasta.

Observation and Variations: This sounds like a fancy dish, but all it takes is pan-frying breaded chicken then making a reduction with lemon juice and capers to serve with it. If the word "reduction" intimidates you, all it means is boiling a liquid until enough has boiled off that its total volume is reduced. So it's nothing fancy at all! You can use that same lemon-caper reduction for salmon or in veal scallopini. It works with several different proteins.

Meatloaf

Meatloaf is a really economical but filling dish. Everyone in my family always wanted me to make meatloaf because they wanted to make meatloaf sandwiches the next day. A meatloaf sandwich with mayo is a game changer! If I make meatloaf for myself, I'll have a slice for dinner, then put it in the fridge to chill for sandwiches the rest of the week.

2 lbs. ground beef (or 1 lb. ground beef and 1 lb. ground pork)

1 tbsp. butter

1 tbsp. olive oil

1 medium onion, finely-chopped

3 garlic cloves, minced

2 eggs

3 tbsp. ketchup

3 tbsp. parsley, finely chopped

¾ c. panko breadcrumbs

⅓ c. milk

1½ tsp. salt

1 tsp. freshly-ground black pepper

3 tbsp. Worcestershire sauce

Glaze

½ c. ketchup

1½ tsp. white vinegar

1½ tsp. brown sugar

½ tsp. garlic powder

½ tsp. onion powder

Pinch salt

Pinch pepper

Preheat the oven to 375 degrees Fahrenheit.

In a skillet, sauté the onions in the butter and olive oil until translucent. Set the onions aside to completely cool. Line a loaf pan with parchment paper and set aside. In a large bowl, place all the ingredients and mix well. Put the mixture into loaf pan and bake for one hour. In a small bowl, mix the ketchup, brown sugar, white vinegar, garlic, and onion powders. Pour over top of the meatloaf and place back in the oven for thirty minutes. If you do not have a loaf pan, you can form it into a loaf on a cookie sheet or in a baking dish and follow the above directions.

Cocoa-Spiced Steaks with Red Wine Chocolate Sauce

You'll feel like a real kitchen show-off when you bring these to the table!

2 tsp. unsweetened cocoa powder

2 tsp. kosher salt

1½ tsp. granulated sugar

1 tsp. sweet paprika

¼ tsp. cayenne pepper or chipotle powder

2 tsp. coffee grounds

2 ribeye or strip steaks

¼ c. unsalted butter, softened

2 tsp. canola oil or vegetable oil

⅓ c. chopped shallot

1 tsp. all-purpose flour

½ c. dry red wine

1 c. beef or chicken broth

½ tbsp. chopped flat leaf parsley

Stir together cocoa powder, salt, sugar, paprika, cayenne, and coffee grounds in a small bowl and set aside. Pat the steaks dry with the paper towel and rub one tablespoon cocoa mixture all over the steaks. Let stand, uncovered, at room temperature for fifteen minutes. While waiting for the steaks, stir together the butter and remaining cocoa mixture in a small bowl. Divide evenly into four portions and set aside. Heat the oil in a large skillet over high heat. The oil should ripple and almost smoke. Add the steaks and cook until browned in spots (1-1½ minutes). Flip steaks on the other side with a pair of tongs and cook until browned in spots (1-1½ minutes). Brown the edges of the steaks for 15-30 seconds. Reduce the heat to medium and continue cooking the steaks, turning often, until they are a rich dark brown. Add one of the four butter and cocoa portions to the skillet.

Cook over medium heat until the steaks are coated in melted butter, and a meat thermometer in the thickest portion registers 125-130 Fahrenheit for medium rare, or 135-140 Fahrenheit for medium, for 1-3 minutes. Transfer steaks to a plate and tent with aluminum foil. Let them rest until ready to serve. Discard all but one tablespoon drippings in skillet, reduce heat to medium low, and stir shallots into the reserved drippings. Cook, whisking constantly until shallot is translucent, about one minute. Coat the shallots with the flour, whisk in wine, and bring to boil. Boil, undisturbed until thickened, one to two minutes. Whisk in the broth and any juices from the steak plate, increase heat to high, and bring to a vigorous simmer. Simmer, whisking occasionally until sauce reduces by almost half. Sauce should lightly coat the back of a metal spoon, about six minutes. Remove skillet from heat and whisk in two of the remaining butter-cocoa portions. Add the parsley and stir. Place steaks on serving dishes, spoon the sauce over, and top evenly with the remaining butter and cocoa mix.

Main Dish Casseroles

Casseroles are great convenience foods. They're easy to prepare and easy to keep warm if you think some folks might arrive late for dinner. For a single person who lives alone, they can be portioned out for future meals and will reheat well. Plus, most casseroles are better the next day anyway!

The tendency when you're alone is not to cook at all and rely on fast food. But casseroles are comfort foods that satisfy your desire for a good meal. Now that it's only me at home, I will sometimes make something like a lasagne or cheese chicken spaghetti on Sunday afternoon, and portion it to eat all week. If I also make a big salad on Sunday, I've prepared myself a full meal every day. I think a vacuum sealer is a great blessing for any busy family. I've made casseroles, cooled them, then vacuum-sealed individual portions for future use. I can also freeze some portions for another week, and I can use those for variety.

Five-Ingredient Chicken Pot Pie

I used to work with a scrub tech who ate every meal out. She could not boil water. I brought her one of my chicken pot pies, and she went crazy. I told her: You're going to go home and make this yourself. "No way!" she told me.

I gave her this recipe and sent her shopping. She called me three times from the grocery store, texting me photos of each item she bought to make sure she was getting the right ingredients. When she got home, she took a picture of the premade pie crust after she unrolled it. She put in the filling and took a picture. When it came out of the oven, she sent me a picture. She could not believe she had created something that delicious with only five ingredients. You can have your own chicken pot pie on the table in just over thirty minutes. What a yummy relief on a busy week night!

Premade pie crust (see biscuit section in refrigerated case)

2 c. shredded rotisserie chicken

One 10.5 oz. can cream of potato soup

⅓ c. milk

1 c. mixed frozen vegetables

½ tsp. salt

¼ tsp. pepper

Preheat the oven to 425 degrees Fahrenheit.

The premade pie crust packages come with two crusts. Set the package on the counter so they'll warm a bit from the room temperature. That way, they won't crack when you unroll them and put them in the pie pan. Place the first crust in the bottom of a pie pan and press down. In a bowl, mix the chicken, the soup, the milk, the vegetables, and the salt and pepper, stirring until well combined. (The vegetables can still be frozen at this point!) Place the ingredients in the pie pan over the first crust and place the second crust over the top. Crimp the edges all around the edge of the plate. With a sharp knife, make three or four vent holes in the center of the top crust. Bake for thirty minutes.

Tip: What should you do if your pie crust cracks? Dip your finger in water and rub it over the crack to seal it. Like magic!

Variations: You could substitute the chicken in this recipe with cooked and cubed beef, ham, bacon, or a combination of all three.

Ground Beef and Ravioli Casserole

One 24 oz. jar marinara sauce

One 9 oz. package frozen cheese ravioli

1 lb. ground beef

1 small onion, diced

1 bell pepper, diced

2 c. freshly shredded mozzarella cheese

¼ c. grated parmesan cheese (more if you like)

1 tsp. crushed red pepper flakes

Preheat the oven to 400 degrees Fahrenheit.

In a large skillet, over medium heat, brown ground beef until crumbly. Add onion and bell pepper, and continue to cook until the onion is translucent. Spray a 9x13-inch baking dish with non-stick spray. Place one-third jar of marinara sauce evenly on the bottom of the dish. Follow with a layer of ravioli and then a layer of ground beef. Sprinkle one-third of the mozzarella over the top. Continue this sequence for two more layers, ending with mozzarella. Sprinkle the parmesan and red pepper flakes over the top and cover with foil. Cook for twenty minutes. Remove the foil and cook for an additional twenty minutes, or until cheese is browned and bubbly.

Pizza Casserole

2 c. short dry pasta (shape is your choice)

1 lb. ground beef

One 14 oz. jar pasta sauce

One 4 oz. can tomato sauce

4 oz. button mushrooms, sliced

1 lb. shredded mozzarella cheese

Preheat the oven to 350 degrees Fahrenheit.

In a large saucepan, bring five quarts of water to a boil, seasoning with two tablespoons salt. Cook pasta for eight minutes until *al dente*. Strain and set aside. In a large skillet, brown the ground beef until crumbly. Add the mushrooms and cook for 4-5 more minutes. In a large bowl, mix ground beef, pasta, pasta sauce, tomato sauce, and mushrooms. Stir together to blend. Spray a 9x13" baking dish with a non-stick cooking spray. Put one-third of the ground beef mixture into the bottom of the casserole dish, layering with one-third of the mozzarella cheese. Continue layering this way, ending with cheese on top. Cover with foil, and bake for thirty-five minutes. Remove the foil and cook for ten more minutes.

Ham and Beans

A lot of Southern cooking is about taking a small amount of meat and stretching it out, because like some other cultures, meat has often been hard to come by. There was a time, especially during the Depression, where all you might have for meat was the ham hock, so you'd boil it until all the meat fell off, then add the beans and flavorings. Your protein came from the beans and the flavor came from the ham. Basically, this is a ham and navy bean soup. It's good served with sauteed greens and cornbread, and I've included recipes for those in other chapters.

8 c. water

1 lb. dried Great Northern beans, sorted and rinsed

½ tsp. salt

1 medium yellow onion, chopped

4 cloves garlic, minced

1 tsp. mustard powder

2 bay leaves

1 ham hock

2 c. baked ham, cubed (ham steak is also a good choice)

Freshly-ground black pepper to taste

In a large Dutch oven, over high heat, bring the water and the dried beans to a boil. Boil vigorously for ten minutes, add the salt, remove from the heat and set aside for at least sixty minutes. Add the onion, garlic, mustard powder, bay leaves, and ham hock. Bring back to the boil over high heat, reduce the heat to a simmer, and cook for one and a half hours. Remove the ham hock, let it cool, and shred the cooled meat. Add back to the pot along with the cubed ham and simmer for an additional thirty minutes, or until the beans are tender.

Southern Main Dishes

My friend Terrance grew up in Minnesota, but he is of Indian descent. When he started working in North Carolina, he fell in love with Southern fried foods. Fried catfish, Southern fried chicken, chicken-fried steak. . .he couldn't get enough of them! So these are some of the Southern recipes he loved that I taught him to cook. I also introduced him to hushpuppies, which are among my favorite things. No one puts jalapeños in hushpuppies but me, and he went wild over those. You'll find my hushpuppy recipe as well as my Southern-style cornbread in the Breads and Quick Breads chapter. One of these Southern Mains makes a meal, together with one of those breads, and a side like Mixed Greens, Sweet Potato Casserole, or Cheesy Grits (all in the Side Dishes chapter).

Fried Catfish

1 c. buttermilk

1 tsp. salt

½ tsp. pepper

1 lb. catfish filets, cut into nuggets or strips

1½ c. fine cornmeal

½ c. all-purpose flour

½ tsp. garlic powder

½ tsp. onion powder

1 c. vegetable oil

Pour buttermilk into a resealable one-gallon plastic bag. Add salt and pepper. Add catfish nuggets, seal the bag, and massage the bag to coat. Place the bag in refrigerator and marinate for at least two hours up to overnight. In a medium-sized mixing bowl, combine the cornmeal, flour, garlic powder, and onion powder. Pour the dry ingredients into a shallow baking dish and dredge fish nuggets in the mixture, completely coating all sides. Alternatively, you could put the dry mix into a paper bag and gently shake to coat the fish. In a large skillet, heat the vegetable oil to 375 degrees Fahrenheit. Working in batches, fry the fish until golden brown and crispy on all sides.

Menu Suggestion: A classic Southern dinner, this dish is very good served with coleslaw, French fries, and buttermilk jalapeño hushpuppies. Be sure to serve hot sauce and lots of tartar sauce on the side!

Southern Fried Chicken

3 lb. chicken legs and thighs, skin on

1 qt. buttermilk

1 tbsp. hot sauce

1 tbsp. salt

3 tsp. freshly-ground black pepper, divided

3 c. all-purpose flour

2 tsp. salt

1 tsp. garlic powder

1 tsp. onion powder

1 tsp. paprika

Vegetable oil for frying (amount varies)

Into a one-gallon resealable plastic bag, place chicken, buttermilk, 1 tbsp. salt, 1½ tsp. pepper, and hot sauce. Seal the bag and massage to evenly coat the meat. Place in refrigerator and marinate for at least four hours, preferably overnight. After marinating, remove the chicken from the refrigerator and place the pieces on a wire baking rack. Allow to sit in place for thirty minutes. Heat one inch of oil in a large Dutch oven or a large cast-iron skillet to 350 degrees Fahrenheit. In a large bowl, whisk flour, salt, remaining pepper, garlic, onion powder, and paprika. Combine thoroughly. Pour dry ingredients into a paper bag and add the chicken, shaking gently to coat all surfaces. Working in batches, fry the chicken in the oil for about fifteen minutes, until it is crispy, browned, and the internal temperature, measured near the bone, is 160 degrees. Place cooked pieces into a 200-degree oven to remain hot while the remaining chicken cooks.

Chicken Fried Steak

4 cube steaks (about ½ lb. each)

2 ¼ c. all-purpose flour, divided

1 tsp. salt

1 tsp. freshly-ground black pepper

2 tsp. baking powder

1 tsp. baking soda

1½ c. buttermilk

3 tsp. hot sauce

1 large egg

1½ tsp. garlic powder

3 c. vegetable shortening for frying

4 c. milk

Salt and pepper to taste

Using a meat mallet, pound the steaks to one fourth-inch thickness. You may want to cover with plastic wrap first. Place two cups of flour into a shallow dish. In a second shallow dish, whisk salt, pepper, baking powder, and baking soda together. Add buttermilk, hot sauce, egg, and garlic powder. Whisk briskly to combine. This is a double-breading process. First, dredge each steak in the flour. Next, give it a dip in the buttermilk, holding it over the bowl to catch any drips. Dredge again in the flour and place on a wire baking rack. Allow to set for twenty minutes to seal the coating. Meanwhile, heat your shortening to 325 degrees. Fry steak, in batches, if necessary 3-5 minutes on each side. Move to a paper towel-lined plate to drain excess oil. Cover with foil to keep warm while you make gravy to go over top.

Gravy

Pour cooking liquid from skillet, reserving ¼ cup. Be sure to leave the crispy bits in the bottom of the pan. Put the reserved shortening into the skillet over medium-low heat and add the flour, whisking to lift up the crispy bits. Cook until flour is lightly browned and has a sandy consistency. Pour in milk and, whisk vigorously, cook for about seven minutes, until thickened. Season with salt and pepper to taste and pour over steaks. Rejoice!

Pasta Main Dishes

From our mac and cheese days as children to the more sophisticated Alfredo and lasagnas of adulthood, pasta can be as simple as a bowl of buttered noodles with parmesan, or as elaborate as one chooses. Sauces can be rustic, simple, or as complicated as one is willing to take the time for. The many shapes make mixing and matching pasta and sauce an endless adventure. Comfort food at its best!

Cacio e Pepe (Cheese and Pepper)

When I started teaching Terrance how to make pasta dishes, I made him taste the pasta every minute, so he could recognize the stages it would go through as it cooked. I really don't like overcooked pasta, and there's about a thirty-second window when it's just right. Terrance knows how to hit it now!

12 oz. bucatini pasta or spaghetti

2 tbsp. butter

⅔ c. reserved pasta water

½ c. finely grated parmesan cheese, plus more for garnish

½ tsp. black pepper

In a large pot, boil two quarts of water that has been liberally salted (3-4 tbsp.). Reserve two-third cup of the pasta water, set aside, and drain pasta into a colander. Put the pasta back into the pot it was boiled in and add the butter and the pasta water, stirring just until butter is melted. Add the grated cheese and pepper, and toss until the creamy sauce forms. Garnish with additional grated cheese and enjoy!

Spaghetti

12 oz. spaghetti noodles

1 lb. ground beef

2 tbsp. salt (for boiling pasta) and 2 tsp. salt (for seasoning ground beef)

1 tsp. pepper

1½ tsp. Italian seasoning

1 medium yellow onion, diced

1 green, red, or yellow bell pepper, diced

8 oz. white mushrooms, sliced

One 14.5 oz. can diced, fire-roasted tomatoes

One 4 oz. can diced, mild green chilies (if desired)

1 c. red wine (optional)

Large pot of boiling, salted water

2 c. freshly-grated parmesan cheese

In a large skillet over medium heat, brown ground beef until it is crumbly and evenly browned. Discard any unwanted fat and return to heat. Add the two teaspoons of salt, pepper, and Italian seasoning, and stir to mix. Add the onion, bell pepper, and mushrooms, and cook until the onions are translucent. If using the green chilies, add them now. Simmer for thirty minutes.

While the sauce is simmering, bring the pot of water to the boil, add the two tablespoons of salt, then add pasta. Cook approximately 10-12 minutes or until pasta is *al dente*. Drain into a colander.

Serving: Here you have two choices. You can either place the noodles on individual plates and ladle the sauce over them or simply add the noodles to the sauce, stirring it all together. Each individual can add as much parmesan over top as desired.

Menu Suggestion: This spaghetti is best served with a tossed salad as a starter and a loaf of crusty bread. In a pinch, especially on busy weeknights, you can substitute a jar of your favorite sauce for the tomatoes, and just add the vegetables and further seasoning.

Cheesy Chicken Spaghetti

This recipe starts on the stovetop but it ends up in the oven in the form of a casserole. It is hearty, filling, and feeds a crowd.

12 oz. spaghetti noodles

5 qt. boiling water

2 tbsp. salt

2 cans cream of chicken soup, undiluted

One 10 oz. can Ro-Tel tomatoes (you choose the heat level)

4 oz. cream cheese

½ c. sour cream

¼ c. chicken broth

2 c. cheddar cheese, grated and divided

1 tsp. garlic powder

1 tsp. onion powder

½ tsp. salt

¼ tsp. ground black pepper

Pinch of red pepper flakes

2 c. shredded chicken (leftover or from a rotisserie chicken is fine!)

Fresh parsley for garnish

Preheat the oven to 350 degrees Fahrenheit.

In a large pot, bring water to a boil and add salt. Add pasta and cook for approximately eight minutes until it begins to bend but not cooked through. Test the pasta before the usual ten-minute cooking so it is not overcooked in the oven. Drain pasta into colander and set aside for a minute. Reserving one cup of the cheddar cheese, put all other ingredients into the pot the pasta was cooked in, heat and stir until the cheeses are melted, and everything is well blended. Pour into a 9x13" baking dish that has been sprayed with non-stick vegetable oil and cover with remaining cheddar cheese. Cover with aluminum foil and bake for 20-30 minutes. Remove casserole from oven, remove the aluminum foil, and place back in the oven for another ten minutes.

Lasagna

There are several directions that you can go with lasagna. You can do a veggie lasagna with a bechamel sauce, or you can go for a hearty meat sauce with a tomato base. You have the choice to cook the noodles first, stuff them and roll them up, topping with sauce and cheese, and then popping them in the oven to bake. One excellent time saver is to use pasta noodles that you do not have to precook. These are just laid in a baking dish layered with sauce and cheese for several layers, then topped with sauce and cheese, and into the oven they go.

Lasagna with Meat Sauce

1 box "no boil" lasagna noodles

1 lb. ground beef

1½ tsp. salt

1½ tsp. dried Italian seasoning

Two 14.5 oz. cans diced, Italian seasoned, fire-roasted tomatoes

1 medium yellow onion, diced

8 oz. white mushrooms, thinly-sliced

2 c. grated mozzarella cheese

½ c. parmesan cheese, finely-grated

1 tsp. pepper

Preheat the oven to 350 degrees Fahrenheit.

In a large skillet, brown the ground beef until it is crumbly and evenly brown. Add the salt, pepper, and Italian seasoning, and stir to blend. Add the onion and the mushrooms and cook until the onion is translucent. Simmer mixture for thirty minutes.

Assembly

Spray a 9x13" pan with non-stick vegetable spray. Spread a small amount of sauce on the bottom of the pan so that the noodles will stay in one place. Next, lay the dry noodles in one layer to fill the bottom of the pan. Ladle a layer of the sauce over the dry noodles. Cover with one third of the mozzarella. Continue these layers to the top of the pan, finishing with sauce and the remaining mozzarella at the end. Sprinkle with the parmesan cheese, cover with aluminum foil, and bake for fifty minutes. Take from the oven, remove the foil cover, and place back in the oven for another ten minutes. Remove the lasagna and let it rest for five minutes before slicing and serving.

Vegetable Lasagna

1 box "no boil" lasagna noodles

3 c. frozen broccoli and cauliflower mixture, thawed

2 c. grated mozzarella cheese

½ c. finely-grated parmesan cheese

Bechamel Sauce

5 tbsp. butter

¼ c. all-purpose flour

1 qt. milk, room temperature

1½ tsp. salt

¼ tsp. grated nutmeg

In a medium saucepan, over medium heat, melt the butter. Sprinkle the flour evenly over the butter, and, using a whisk, blend evenly. The whisk is important as it keeps lumps out. Cook for seven minutes and then add the milk slowly, whisking all the while. Bring to a low boil and cook for fifteen minutes until all the floury raw taste is gone. Remove from the heat and add the salt and the nutmeg.

Assembly

Spray a 9x13" casserole dish with non-stick vegetable spray. Spread a small amount of the bechamel sauce on the bottom of the pan. Lay the uncooked pasta noodles in a single layer in the bottom of the pan. Next, layer one third of the vegetable mixture and cover with one third of the bechamel sauce and one third of the mozzarella cheese. Repeat layers to the top of the pan, ending with bechamel and mozzarella. Evenly sprinkle parmesan cheese over the top. Cover with foil and bake at 350 Fahrenheit for forty-five minutes. When removed from the oven, remove the foil, and place back in the oven for ten more minutes to brown the cheese on top. Allow to rest for ten minutes before serving.

Spaghetti alla Carbonara

12 oz. dry spaghetti noodles

2 tbsp. of salt

2 large eggs and 2 egg yolks, room temperature

⅔ c. grated parmesan cheese, packed

Coarse ground black pepper

1 tbsp. olive oil

3½ oz. pancetta or bacon, chopped into small dice

In a large pot, place five quarts of water. When water comes to a boil add two tablespoon salt, then add spaghetti. Cook spaghetti for about ten minutes until not quite *al dente*. Drain into a colander. Fill a large bowl with hot water to warm it for serving and set aside. Mix eggs, yolks, parmesan, and black pepper in a large bowl and set aside. Fry pancetta or bacon in a skillet with one tablespoon olive oil until cooked but not yet crispy. Add the drained pasta to the skillet and cook for one minute. Empty and dry the serving bowl and set aside. Remove the skillet from the heat. Add the egg mixture to the pasta-filled skillet and stir vigorously to blend, about one minute. (The residual heat will temper the eggs, melt the cheese and make a creamy sauce.) Pour mixture into bowl and serve while hot.

Variation: If you're a fan of Romano cheese, you can do one-third cup Romano cheese and one-third cup parmesan.

Egg Main Dishes

We often think of eggs as breakfast food, but omelets, quiches, and egg-based vegetable tarts are also excellent main dishes for a lighter lunch or dinner. All of these are great ways to get veggies into your family.

No-Crust Quiche

This is a very versatile recipe that offers many chances to make it your own. With the base of baking mix, eggs and milk, the fillings are endless. Mix and match and try your own imagination when using this recipe.

1 c. cubed ham

1 c. broccoli florets (you can use frozen and thawed)

½ c. diced onion

2 c. grated cheddar cheese

4 eggs, beaten

¾ c. baking mix (such as Bisquick or Pioneer)

1½ c. milk

Preheat the oven to 400 degrees Fahrenheit.

In a 9x13" baking dish, scatter ham across the bottom. Evenly distribute broccoli florets and onion in the dish. Cover with cheddar cheese. Blend together the eggs, baking mix and milk, and pour evenly over the vegetables. Bake for thirty minutes until the top is browned. Remove from oven and let rest for five minutes before serving.

Variations: This quiche can be made with any mixture of vegetables and meats that you prefer. Spinach, bacon, and Swiss cheese are one suggestion. Just experiment and you'll soon find your favorite.

Breakfast Vegetable Tart

12 large eggs

1 c. freshly-grated sharp cheddar cheese

1 c. broccoli, fresh or frozen

1 c. bell pepper, diced

1 c. yellow onion, diced

2 tsp. garlic powder

2 tsp. onion powder

½ tsp. salt

¼ c. chopped flat leaf parsley

Preheat the oven to 350 degrees Fahrenheit.

Spray an 8" or 9" baking dish with non-stick spray and set aside. In a large bowl, crack the eggs, and, with a fork, beat to combine yolks and whites. (You could choose to lightly sauté the vegetables in olive oil, but it isn't necessary.) Combine the vegetables, cheese, parsley, and eggs, and stir well, then pour into the prepared baking dish. Bake for thirty minutes or until eggs are fully cooked. Cool on a wire rack.

Tip: My favorite toppings are sliced avocado or sour cream.

Omelets

Omelets can be one person's dream dish and another person's total frustration. But, in the end, they just take practice and attention to technique. You must be willing to forgive your mistakes, show yourself a little grace, and try again. I strongly encourage you to practice until you master the art of an omelet because their possibilities are endless.

When I make an omelet, I prepare the pan with a half-and-half mixture of butter and vegetable oil. Butter has a good flavor, but burns quickly. Vegetable oil has a higher smoking point, giving you more time to set the omelet before you flip it.

Basic Omelet

2 large eggs

2 oz. milk or water

½ tsp. salt

¼ tsp. pepper

2 tbsp. butter

2 tbsp. vegetable oil

In a medium bowl, beat eggs until well blended. Add milk or water and beat a second time. Add salt and pepper and stir. Spray a small skillet with nonstick vegetable oil. In the skillet, over medium heat, heat the vegetable oil and the butter until the butter has melted and becomes bubbly. Pour the egg mixture into the pan and allow the outside edges to set. When the outer edges have solidified a little, begin to lift the edges up letting the wet mixture slide underneath. Continue to go around the outer edge of the pan lifting at the edges and allowing the unset egg mixture to run underneath to cook. When there are no longer any liquid eggs on the surface, put any additions along the center (like vegetables or cheese; see Omelet Variations). Fold the omelet into thirds by folding one edge to the center and then folding that over the rest. Flip the folded omelet and cook 1-2 minutes on the other side, then turn onto a plate.

Omelet Variations

Omelets have endless possibilities. They can be plain or be filled with any mixture of vegetables, cooked meats, and/or cheese that you prefer. Spinach, onion, green pepper, green chilies, mushrooms, salsa, and avocados are excellent additions. You may also use a mixture of bacon, chopped ham, or crumbled sausage. Cheeses that work well include cheddar, Brie, Colby jack, pepper jack, and Swiss. I like bell pepper, mushrooms, baby spinach, and cheddar myself.

Omelets are limited only by your imagination, so go wild!

Super Speedy Weekday Omelet

If you want to make an omelet without dirtying a pan, you can make an omelet in your microwave. The ingredients are the same as above. Mix your eggs with milk, cream, or water, and put in any vegetables you want and cheese. Stir it all together, pour into a quart ziplock bag, and zip it not quite closed so you leave a very small steam vent. Put the ziplock bag in the microwave on a plate, micro high for one minute, flip, and micro high one minute more. When you pour it out onto a plate, it will fold just like one you make in a pan. This is a good breakfast with enough protein to keep you full till lunch, and the only dish you don't dirty any cooking dishes.

Huevos Rancheros

This dish couldn't be easier, and it's a great breakfast for one. Cook more eggs if more people are eating.

Two eggs

Green Chili (see Main Dishes)

Shredded cheese

Cook two eggs any way you like. Put them on a plate and top them with green chili and shredded cheese. Serve with tortillas on the side instead of toast or biscuits.

Soups and Stews

Think of falling leaves. Think wind and rain. Think of snow days. And when you think about all these things, also think inside, fireplaces, and comfort food. Nothing is more comforting than a hot soup or hearty stew on a cold day. Whether you are a purist and like to make stovetop or oven soup, or you're a timesaver who can't imagine life without a crockpot or instant pot, these recipes are simple and sufficient on their own as a meal. However, the addition of a side salad and a warm loaf of crusty bread only add to the enjoyment!

White Wine Coq Au Vin

(Chicken in wine)

This classic, rustic stew, created in France is comfort at its best! You probably have seen *Coq Au Vin* made with red wine. I like white wine with chicken, so that's how I make it. Cook with wine that you like to drink! When I was teaching Terrance to cook, I always served with the meal the wine we had cooked the dish in. It doesn't take an expensive wine to make an excellent dish. In my opinion, one of the greatest cooking wines is Two Buck Chuck from Trader Joe's. When you choose an economical cooking wine, you can experiment on something brand new without breaking the bank.

2 tsp. olive oil

4 oz. pancetta, cut into half-inch pieces

One 3½–4 lb. whole chicken, cut into 10 pieces

Kosher salt and freshly-ground black pepper

One 8-oz. package white button or cremini mushrooms, quartered

2 medium onions, chopped

2 cloves garlic, chopped

2 tbsp. all-purpose flour

1 c. dry white wine

1 c. chicken stock

2 tbsp. Dijon mustard

¼ c. fresh tarragon, chopped (for serving)

Bouquet Garni

6 sprigs thyme (1 tbsp. dried)

2 bay leaves

Make the bouquet garni by tying these herbs into a small square of cheesecloth.

Preheat the oven to 350 degrees Fahrenheit.

Heat oil in a large Dutch oven over medium heat. Add pancetta and cook, stirring occasionally, until browned, 2-4 minutes. Transfer to a paper towel-lined plate, using a slotted spoon. Season chicken with salt and pepper and cook, skin side down, until golden, 5-7 minutes. Transfer the chicken to a plate and set aside. Increase heat to medium high. Add mushrooms and cook 6 to 8 minutes until browned. Reduce heat to medium, then to low, and add onions, garlic. Cook until light golden brown and tender, 8-9 minutes, stirring occasionally. Add flour and cook for one minute, stirring constantly. Add the remaining stock, mustard, and bouquet garni, and gradually add in the wine, stirring constantly. Bring to a simmer. Add back to the pan the pancetta and the chicken with the skin sides up. Cover the pot and place in the oven. Cook for 1.25-1.5 hours and thirty minutes until chicken is cooked through. Discard bouquet garni. Serve topped with tarragon.

Serving Suggestion: I love to serve the same wine a dish is cooked in. Of course, if you're serving dinner with a very expensive wine, you might choose a bottle of Two Buck Chuck to cook with. . .I would!

Guinness Beef Stew

2 tbsp. olive oil

3 lb. beef chuck roast well-trimmed and cut into two-inch pieces

Kosher salt and freshly-ground black pepper

2 medium onions, cut into one-inch thick wedges

4 cloves garlic, chopped

1 lb. medium carrots, cut into one-inch pieces

3 tbsp. all-purpose flour

One 12-oz. can Guinness extra stout or other stout beer

3 c. chicken stock

One 6 oz. can tomato paste

1 lb. Yukon gold potatoes cut into one-inch pieces

8 sprigs of thyme (4 tsp. dried)

2 bay leaves

½ c. fresh flat leaf parsley, chopped

Heat oil in a Dutch oven over medium high heat. Season beef with salt and pepper and dredge in the flour. Cook, in batches, turning occasionally, until browned, 4-5 minutes, adding more oil, if needed. Reduce heat to medium. Add 1½ c. chicken stock, cover and cook, simmering for one hour. After one hour, add onion and cook for 4-6 minutes. Add garlic and carrots and cook, stirring occasionally, until starting to soften, 3-5 minutes. Add Guinness and cook, scraping up any browned bits until starting to thicken for one minute, then add stock and tomato paste and stir to combine. Add thyme springs and bay leaves. Remove lid and cook, uncovered, until beef is very tender, with 30 minutes left to cook, add potatoes. Discard thyme sprigs and bay leaves. Season with salt and pepper. Serve sprinkled with parsley.

Beef Stroganoff

Stroganoff is another great cold-weather food. It is hearty, rich, and filling. Served with a garden salad and a warm, crusty baguette, it's a perfect winter meal.

12 oz. extra-wide egg noodles

5 qt. boiling water, seasoned with two tbsp. salt

2 lb. stew meat

1½ tsp. salt

1 tsp. ground black pepper

½ c. flour

3 tbsp. olive oil

1 medium yellow onion, diced

3 cloves garlic, minced

2 c. chicken stock

¼ c. ketchup

8 oz. mushrooms, thinly-sliced

8 oz. sour cream

1 tbsp. poppy seed, if desired

Season stew meat with salt and pepper. Dredge in flour and cook in olive oil over medium heat until browned on all sides. Add the onion, garlic, chicken stock and ketchup and simmer for two hours until meat is well-done and soft.

Bring the salted water to a boil and cook the egg noodles until they're *al dente*. Drain into a colander and set aside.

Now to the stew meat, add the mushrooms and cook for 5-10 minutes. Stir in the noodles and remove from heat. Stir in the sour cream, and if using, the poppy seed.

Oxtails

I think of this as a very rustic stew. Oxtails used to be a throw-away kind of meat you'd get cheap or free at the butcher. Now, of course, you pay a good price for this specialty meat. If you cook this stew right, the meat will fall right off the bones when you serve it!

2 lb. oxtails, cut into two-inch pieces

1 c. all-purpose flour

1 medium yellow onion, finely-diced

1 c. thinly-sliced scallions, white and light green parts, save the dark tops for garnish

5 medium garlic cloves, diced

2 fresh Scotch bonnet chili peppers, finely-minced

⅓ c. packed light brown sugar

2 tsp. kosher salt

2 tbsp. soy sauce

1 tbsp. freshly-ground black pepper

1 tbsp. ground allspice

2 tbsp. Worcestershire sauce

2 tbsp. vegetable oil

4 c. beef stock

2 c. red wine

2 sprigs rosemary (2 tsp. dried or 1 tsp. ground)

3 medium carrots, cut into 1½-inch pieces

8 oz. button mushrooms

Preheat the oven to 300 degrees Fahrenheit.

Season the oxtails with salt and pepper and dredge in flour. Discard remaining flour. In a large Dutch oven, heat the vegetable oil until shimmering. Brown the oxtails on all sides, working in batches, if necessary. Remove to a plate and set aside. Lower the heat to medium. Cook onions and scallions in remaining oil until onions are translucent. Add the garlic and the chilis and cook for two minutes. Stir together the brown sugar, kosher salt, soy sauce, pepper, allspice, and Worcestershire sauce. Pour over the oxtails and add the beef stock, red wine, and rosemary. Cover and place into the oven for three hours. Remove from the oven and add the carrots and mushrooms. Place back in the oven and cook for forty-five additional minutes.

Chicken Noodle Soup

This soup is perfect for anyone feeling a little under-the-weather, but that isn't the only excuse you need to make it! The consistency of the Kluski noodles makes it hearty and filling. These are a style of noodles made with twice as much egg as other egg noodles. They're like Amish farmhouse noodles, and they don't disintegrate in the soup. . .they have a bit of a bite to them like pasta.

One 3-4 lb. whole chicken

Water to cover

2 tbsp. Better than Bouillon (chicken-flavored)

Kosher salt

Freshly-ground black pepper

1 celery stick, cut into thirds

1 carrot, quartered

One 8 oz. bag Kluski egg noodles

Season chicken with salt and pepper. Place in a large pot, covering it with water. Add bouillon and cook over medium heat until chicken meat starts to fall off the bone. Remove chicken from pot and set aside to cool. Remove and discard celery and carrot. When chicken is cool enough to handle, shred the meat, discarding the bones. Return chicken to pot and bring to a rolling bowl. When boiling, add noodles, and cook for fifteen minutes. Serve hot.

Speed Tip: I prefer to cook my own chicken, but you could do a shortcut with a rotisserie chicken. If you do, then replace the water in the recipe with thirty-two ounces of prepared chicken broth.

Avgolemono

1 whole 3-lb. chicken

½ c. uncooked white rice or orzo pasta

Salt and freshly-ground black pepper to taste

Three large eggs, beaten

2 medium lemons, juiced

Rinse the chicken inside and out and place in a pot big enough to allow room for movement it as it cooks. Cover with water, about one inch over the top. Season with two-teaspoon salt and one-teaspoon black pepper. Over medium heat, bring to a boil, covered. When chicken reaches a boil, reduce heat to low and let cook for forty-five minutes to an hour until the chicken pulls easily from the bone. Remove the chicken from the pot to cool. Add rice to the pot and cook until tender, which takes about twenty minutes. Whisk the lemon and eggs together and set aside. Remove the chicken from the bones. When rice has finished cooking, turn off the heat. Temper the eggs by slowly adding a large ladle full of the hot cooking liquid into the bowl with the eggs, stirring briskly with a whisk. Slowly pour the egg mixture into the pot, stirring continuously so the eggs will not scramble and you'll get a silky smooth soup. Add the chicken back to the pot and serve.

Chicken Tortilla Soup

I like spicy soups like this one because spiciness makes the food even more warming on a cool day. Some people cook the tortilla strips in the soup, but I like the crunch when they're just sprinkled on top. I'm a salty-crunchy person and I'll take these flavors over sweet any day! This a great make-ahead meal to have for a week of lunches.

3 tbsp. olive oil

1 medium onion, peeled and chopped

⅔ c. fresh chopped cilantro, divided

4 cloves garlic, minced

One 14.5 oz. can diced, fire-roasted tomatoes

4 skinless chicken thighs

1 tsp. ground cumin

2 tsp. chili powder

½ tsp. chipotle chili powder

2 bay leaves

2 carrots, cut into thin rounds

One 4 oz. can diced green chilies (Hatch, if available)

One 7 oz. can Fiesta corn

One 15 oz. can black beans

2 c. shredded Monterey Jack cheese

2 avocados, diced

1 bag thin tortilla strips

In a large saucepan or Dutch oven, heat the oil to medium. Add the onions, one-third cup cilantro, and garlic. Sauté until onions are translucent. Stir in the chicken broth, tomatoes, spices and three-fourth teaspoon salt. Add the chicken thighs, pushing them to the bottom of the pot, and bring the pot to a boil. Add the carrots. return to a boil and then lower the heat to medium and cook for twelve minutes. Add the chilies, corn, beans, and heat through. Remove the chicken thighs, and when cool enough to handle, shred the meat. Stir in 1 cup Monterey Jack cheese, leaving the rest as garnish. Ladle the soup into bowls and top with your choice of accompaniments, fresh cilantro, the remaining cheese, avocado and tortilla strips.

Speedier Variation: This recipe can be made even faster with the use of rotisserie chicken. If using a rotisserie chicken for this recipe, use thirty-two ounces of commercial chicken stock. Assemble the entire soup and put the shredded chicken in at the end just to warm it through.

Cauliflower Bisque with Brown Butter Croutons

2 c. whole milk

1 small head cauliflower (about a pound), broken into florets

2½ c. chicken stock

¾ lb. Yukon gold potatoes, peeled and chopped

1 small onion, chopped

2 cloves garlic, crushed

4 sprigs thyme (2 tsp. dried)

Kosher salt and freshly-ground black pepper

3 tbsp. unsalted butter

3 c. cubed ciabatta bread

⅓ c. heavy cream

⅓ c. pomegranate seeds

¼ c. chopped chives

In a large saucepan, combine milk, stock, cauliflower, potato, onion, garlic, and thyme. Season with one teaspoon salt and one-half teaspoon pepper. Bring to a boil over medium high heat, then reduce and simmer partly covered, until the vegetables are tender, about twenty minutes. While vegetables are cooking, melt butter in a large skillet over medium heat. Swirling occasionally, cook until golden brown, 2-4 minutes. Add bread, and stirring often, cook until toasted, 10-12 minutes. Sprinkle with salt and pepper. Set aside for serving. Discard the thyme sprigs, then puree the soup until smooth, using an immersion blender. Add cream and pulse to combine. Salt and pepper to taste. Serve topped with croutons, pomegranate seeds, and chives.

French Onion Soup

6 tbsp. unsalted butter

4 sweet onions, thinly-sliced (if you have one, use a mandoline)

2 cloves garlic, minced

1 tbsp. Worcestershire sauce

1½ tbsp. all-purpose flour

1 c. of your favorite beer or red wine

8 c. beef broth

2 bay leaves

4 fresh thyme sprigs, plus more for garnish (2 tsp. dried)

2 tsp. salt to taste

Large pinch of freshly-ground black pepper

1 French baguette, thickly-sliced (about 1½ inch)

1 c. shredded gruyere cheese

1 c. shredded Swiss cheese

Preheat the oven to 250 degrees Fahrenheit.

Thickly slice the baguette and place on a cookie sheet. Toast low and slow for thirty minutes. Remove from oven and set aside. Increase the oven temperature to 400 degrees. In a heavy bottom Dutch oven, over medium heat, melt the butter. Add in thinly-sliced onions and heat on medium low for 30-40 minutes, stirring occasionally. Once the onions are soft and have begun to caramelize on the edges, drizzle beer or wine, and heat on medium low until most of the liquid is evaporated. Sprinkle the flour evenly over the onion slices. Add Worcestershire sauce and bay leaves and cook for 1-3 minutes. Fill the pot with the beef stock, add the thyme, and simmer on low for 30-40 minutes. Salt and pepper to taste. Ladle soup into individual ramekins, place a slice of the toasted bread on top, and cover with the two cheeses that you have mixed. Place the ramekins on a cookie sheet and slide it into the oven, cooking until the cheese is bubbling and brown. Serve immediately.

Roasted Broccoli Soup

6 c. broccoli florets

1 medium red onion, large dice

4 cloves garlic, sliced

2 tbsp. olive oil

1 tsp. salt

½ tsp. pepper

3 c. chicken stock

One ½ c. cheddar cheese

Croutons

Preheat the oven to 425 degrees Fahrenheit.

Place broccoli, onion, garlic, olive oil, salt, and pepper on a cookie sheet and start to coat the vegetables with oil. Roast for forty minutes until the broccoli begins to be a little charred. Set aside a few florets of the broccoli to be used as a garnish later. Remove from the oven. Place, with chicken stock, in a high-speed blender (or place in a stock pot and use an immersion blender). Blend until smooth. In a stock pot, heat on medium until the desired temperature. Serve garnished with broccoli florets, cheddar cheese, and croutons.

New England Clam Chowder

Three 6.5 oz. cans chopped clams in juice

8 oz. clam juice

8 thick center-cut bacon strips, chopped

2 tbsp. butter

2 stalks celery, finely chopped

1 large onion, cut into ¼ inch dice

1½ c. russet potatoes, peeled and cut to ½ inch dice

4 garlic cloves, minced

½ tsp. red pepper flakes (optional)

⅓ c. all-purpose flour

2 c. chicken broth

2 tsp. chicken flavored bouillon

½ tsp. dried oregano

½ tsp. dried parsley

½ tsp. salt

¼ tsp. pepper

¼ tsp. thyme

1 c. heavy cream

Oyster crackers and fresh parsley for garnish, if desired

In a large Dutch oven, over medium heat, cook bacon until browned. With the slotted spoon, remove half the bacon and transfer to a plate lined with paper towel. To the remaining bacon, add one tablespoon butter. Increase the heat to medium high and sauté the onion and celery until the onions are translucent. Add garlic, red pepper flakes, and potatoes, and sauté for thirty seconds. Add flour and cook for an additional minute. Drain the clams into a measuring cup and add clam juice to make two and a half cups. Add chicken broth, clam juice, bouillon, bay leaves, and all other seasonings. Bring to a boil, reduce to a simmer, and simmer for 15-20 minutes until the potatoes are tender. Stir the heavy cream and simmer until heated through. Remove from heat and add clams. Remove and discard bay leaves. Salt and pepper to taste. Garnish with reserved bacon, parsley, and oyster crackers, if desired.

Creamy Tomato Soup

2 tbsp. butter, divided

2 tbsp. olive oil, divided

1 medium onion, very thinly-sliced

3 cloves garlic, smashed

Three 14 oz. cans of whole tomatoes in juice (about 5 cups)

1 c. water

⅔ c. heavy cream

1 tbsp. sugar

¼ tsp. crushed red pepper flakes

¼ tsp. dried oregano

¼ tsp. celery seeds

Kosher salt

Freshly-ground black pepper

Four slices of white country bread, crust trimmed, cut into ¾-inch dice

In a large saucepan, add one tablespoon butter and one tablespoon of olive oil. When the butter has melted, working over medium heat, add the onions and garlic for and sauté for 5-7 minutes, until onions are translucent. Add the tomatoes, water, heavy cream, sugar, pepper flakes, oregano, and celery seeds. Bring to a boil over high heat, breaking up the tomatoes with the back of a spoon. Lower heat to simmer and simmer for ten minutes. Smooth out the soup with the use of a blender or an immersion blender. If using a countertop blender, work in batches. Return to saucepan and reheat, if necessary. In a small skillet, over moderate heat, melt the butter, swirling occasionally until it begins to brown. Scrape the butter into a small bowl and set aside. Into the same skillet, put the remaining olive oil and gently fry the bread cubes until browned, about 6-7 minutes. Add the brown butter and toss. Serve the soup piping hot with croutons on top.

Sausage and Tortellini Soup

1 lb. Italian sausage (hot or mild)

1 medium yellow onion, diced

3 cloves garlic, minced

3 tbsp. flour

1 tsp. dried basil

½ tsp. oregano

1 tsp. hot sauce

½ tsp. mustard powder

½ tsp. crushed red pepper flakes

5 c. chicken broth

2 c. kale, chopped

2 c. tortellini

salt and pepper to taste

If the Italian sausage is in links, remove from the casings. In a large stock pot, brown sausage along with onions, cooking until sausage is browned and onions are translucent. Add the garlic and cook for one minute. Sprinkle the flour over all and cook for 1-2 minutes to cook the raw taste out of the flour. Add the basil, oregano, hot sauce, mustard powder, and red pepper flakes, stirring to combine. Add the five cups of chicken broth and bring to a boil. When broth is at a full boil, add the kale and the tortellini, and cook for three minutes. Serve hot.

Chicken and Wild Rice Soup

1 tbsp. butter

1 tbsp. olive oil

1 medium yellow onion, small dice

2 carrots, thinly-sliced

2 celery stalks, thinly-sliced

5 cloves Garlic, minced

¼ c. all-purpose flour

6 c. chicken stock

1 lb. boneless, skinless chicken breast (or rotisserie chicken)

8 oz. mushrooms, sliced

One ½ tsp. rosemary

2 bay leaves

1 c. uncooked wild rice blend

2 c. milk

2 c. baby spinach, chopped

In a large saucepan, sauté the onions, carrots, and celery over medium heat until the vegetables soften and the onion is translucent, about ten minutes. Add the garlic and heat for another minute. Sprinkle the flour over all and cook for three minutes until the vegetables are coated and begin to brown. If you are using raw chicken breasts, add the chicken stock, chicken, mushrooms, rosemary, bay leaves, and wild rice to the pan and stir. Simmer over low heat for 40-45 minutes, until rice is tender. Stir in milk and spinach and cook for another five minutes. (If you are using rotisserie chicken, you will add it last, just to heat through).

Side Dishes

Often the simplest and quickest side dish is a tossed salad or a bowl of steamed vegetables that you take out of the freezer and microwave. The easiest way to stretch a meal when extra guests show up: Add another quick side. When you have enough time to make the meal more special, here are some favorite side dishes.

Potatoes Au Gratin

2 tbsp. softened butter

4 russet potatoes, scrubbed and dried

One ½ c. heavy cream

½ c. whole milk

4 cloves of garlic, minced

1 tsp. salt

Pepper to taste

One ½ c. freshly-grated sharp cheddar cheese

Preheat the oven to 400 degrees Fahrenheit.

Spread the softened butter all over the bottom of a 9x13" baking dish. Slice the potatoes and then slice the discs into quarters. Whisk the cream, milk, garlic, salt, and pepper together and set aside. Place one third of the potatoes in the baking dish, pouring one third of the cream mixture over. Sprinkle one third of the cheese. Repeat layers twice more, ending with cream. Reserve the last one third of the cheese. Cover with foil and bake for thirty minutes. Remove foil and continue to bake for twenty more minutes, until the potatoes are golden brown and bubbly. Sprinkle remaining cheese over the top and place back in the oven for five minutes until the cheese is melted and bubbly. Allow to rest for ten minutes before serving by spoonfuls.

128

Original Green Bean Casserole

Everyone loves this super-easy side dish casserole, quickly assembled from ingredients in the cupboard. Some families save this for holiday meals, but I love it all the time.

One 10.5 oz. can cream of mushroom soup

½ c. milk

1 tsp. soy sauce

2 cans cut green beans

1½ c. French fried onions, divided

Salt and pepper to taste

Preheat the oven to 350 degrees Fahrenheit.

In a 1½-quart baking dish, combine soup, milk, soy sauce, green beans, and two third-cup onions. Season with salt and pepper. Bake for twenty-five minutes until bubbly. Remove from the oven and top with the remaining French fried onions. Return to the oven and bake for another five minutes or until the onions are browned.

Broccoli, Wild Rice, and Cheese Casserole

You can use white rice in this casserole, but I prefer the texture of the wild rice.

5 tbsp. butter

1 large onion, chopped

16 oz. frozen, chopped broccoli

⅓ c. milk

Two 10.5 oz. cans cream of mushroom soup

3 c. cooked wild rice blend

1½ c. of freshly-grated sharp cheddar cheese

¼ tsp. freshly-ground black pepper

½ tsp. salt

Preheat the oven to 350 degrees Fahrenheit.

Before assembling the other ingredients, cook the rice. In a medium stock pot, place three and one fourth cups of water. Stir in two cups of rice blend and bring to a boil over medium heat. Lower the heat to a simmer and cook for fifty minutes, without removing the lid. Add one tablespoon of butter and wait three minutes to fluff the rice. Using the remaining four tablespoons of butter, in a medium skillet, sauté the onions until translucent. Add the broccoli and sauté until crisp-tender. Stir in the milk, soup, rice, and cheese, cooking and stirring until cheese is melted. Place into an 11x8x2" baking dish and bake for thirty minutes.

Easy Corn Casserole

One 10.5 oz. can cream of mushroom soup

½ c. milk

1 tsp. soy sauce

2 cans cut corn

Salt and pepper to taste

Preheat the oven to 350 degrees Fahrenheit.

In a 1½-quart baking dish, combine soup, milk, soy sauce, green beans, and two-third cup onions. Season with salt and pepper. Bake for twenty-five minutes until bubbly.

Corn and Zucchini Fritters

2 c. all-purpose flour

½ c. sugar

1 tbsp. baking powder

½ tsp. cumin

½ tsp. salt

Freshly-ground black pepper to taste

1 c. milk

¼ c. butter, melted

2 large eggs, beaten

2 c. grated zucchini

One ½ c. fresh corn, cut the kernels from the cob

1 c. shredded cheddar cheese (optional)

4 tbsp. olive or vegetable oil for shallow frying

Mix flour, sugar, baking powder, cumin, salt, and pepper in a large bowl. In a small bowl, mix milk, butter, and eggs, stirring briskly. Add to the dry mixture and whisk together. Stir in zucchini, corn, and cheese (if using), and combine well. In a large skillet, bring the oil to 375 degrees Fahrenheit. Make small cakes, like pancakes, by adding spoonsful of batter to oil in small batches, cooking for about four minutes, turning once halfway through cooking time. Remove to a paper-towel-lined plate. Serve with ranch dressing on the side.

Mexican Corn

Two 15.25 oz. cans whole kernel corn, drained

One 8 oz. package creamed corn

¼ c. butter

One 4 oz. can diced Hatch green chilies

1 tsp. garlic salt

8 oz. shredded cheddar cheese (optional)

In a medium saucepan, combine all ingredients. Over medium heat, cook and stir for about ten minutes, until heated through. Stir constantly when cheese starts to melt.

Creamed Spinach

Three 10 oz. bags fresh spinach, bigger stems removed, and roughly chopped

¼ c. butter

⅓ c. small white onion, minced

3 cloves garlic, minced

1¼ c. heavy cream

6 slices provolone cheese

½ c. freshly-grated parmesan cheese

¼ tsp. freshly-grated nutmeg

Salt and pepper to taste

In a large skillet, over medium heat, add spinach and wilt. Drain in a colander, getting out as much liquid as possible. Set aside. In the same skillet, over medium heat, melt the butter and cook onion and garlic until onion is translucent. Return the spinach to the skillet and add the heavy cream. Cut the provolone into strips and liberally spread over the spinach mixture. Cook, stirring, until cheese is melted. Add parmesan cheese and melt, thickening the dish. Stir in nutmeg. Season with salt and pepper. Serve immediately.

Cooked Cabbage

1 head cabbage, shredded and cored

1 medium yellow onion, diced

4 cloves garlic, minced

8 thick-cut slices bacon, chopped into 1-inch pieces

1½ tsp. salt

1 tsp. freshly-ground black pepper

½ tsp. paprika

½ tsp. garlic powder

½ tsp. onion powder

In a large stock pot or Dutch oven, over medium heat, fry bacon until crispy. Add onions and garlic, and cook until onion is translucent. Add cabbage and cook, stirring for about ten minutes. Add remaining seasonings and cook for thirty minutes.

Mixed Greens

If you're not a Southerner, you may not ever have had this kind of cooked greens. Before we got married, the only cooked green my husband had eaten was spinach from a can. You could have knocked me down with a feather the day he came into the kitchen and asked if I would make a pot of greens for supper!

2 bunches collard greens

2 bunches mustard greens

2 bunches turnip greens

4 c. chicken stock

1 smoked ham hock

1 medium yellow onion, diced

4 cloves garlic, minced

3 tbsp. olive oil

1½ tsp. salt

1 tsp. freshly-ground black pepper

1½ tsp. crushed red pepper flakes

White vinegar (for serving)

Rinse the greens several times to remove all dirt and grit. Remove the stems from the greens and roughly chop. Set aside. In a large stock pot, brown the onions in the olive oil over medium heat until translucent, add garlic, and cook for two more minutes. Pour two cups chicken stock in the pot and then add the ham hock. Cook on medium heat for forty-five minutes, until the meat starts to pull from the bone. Add the greens, salt, pepper, red pepper flakes, and remaining chicken stock. Continue over medium heat until greens are tender. Serve with white vinegar to pour over, as desired.

Sweet Potato Casserole

4 c. peeled, cubed sweet potatoes
(about 4 large potatoes)

2 large eggs, beaten

½ c. granulated sugar

½ c. milk

4 tbsp. butter, softened

½ tsp. vanilla extract

½ tsp. salt

Pecan Topping

½ c. packed brown sugar

⅓ c. all-purpose flour

3 tbsp. butter, softened

½ c. chopped pecans

Preheat the oven to 325 degrees Fahrenheit.

Spray a 9x13" baking dish with non-stick spray. In a medium saucepan, over medium-high heat, boil potatoes, covered with water, for 10-15 minutes, until tender. Drain and place in a large bowl. Mash with hand masher until smooth. Add beaten eggs and mix until evenly combined. Add sugar, milk, butter, vanilla, and salt, and stir until smooth. Pour into prepared pan and set aside to make topping. Mix brown sugar and flour together in a medium bowl until well-blended. Cut in butter with a pastry cutter or a fork, until mixture is the size of peas. Add pecans and mix well. Sprinkle evenly over sweet potato mixture. Bake for twenty minutes until the topping is lightly browned.

Old-Fashioned Cornbread Dressing

Nothing smells better when cooking than cornbread dressing! The smell of sage fills the house and makes guests instantly feel welcomed. My grandmother's dressing had to serve a lot of family members, and still, there were hardly ever leftovers. She made her cornbread earlier in the week, taking it out to crumble and toast in a low oven for a while, to crisp it up. That's a practice I still follow. I like to use a boxed mix that doesn't have much added sugar, like Jiffy Corn Muffin mix.

Cornbread

2 boxes Jiffy Corn Muffin mix

⅔ c. buttermilk

2 eggs

1 tbsp. melted butter

Two 4 oz. cans Hatch diced green chilis (I like HOT!)

Preheat the oven to 400 degrees Fahrenheit.

Mix all above ingredients and pour into a 9x13" baking dish, or a large (10") cast-iron skillet that you have sprayed with non-stick vegetable spray. Bake for twenty minutes, until golden brown. Cool completely, then cover and set aside until time to assemble the dressing.

Jalapeño Dressing

6 c. crumbled cornbread

4 tbsp. butter

2 small yellow onions, diced

1 c. celery, sliced thinly

4 large eggs, beaten

4 c. chicken stock

2 tbsp. ground sage

2 cans five-roastedhot green chilis

1 tsp. ground cumin

½ tsp. chipotle chili powder

Reheat the oven to 250 degrees Fahrenheit, crumble the cornbread, and spread it out on a cookie sheet to toast for thirty minutes.

In a 10" skillet, melt the butter and sauté the onions and celery for about 4-5 minutes until onions are translucent. Pour over crumbled cornbread. Beat the four eggs and stir into the cornbread mixture. Add the chicken stock (you may not need all of the stock, but you want a very wet mixture as the cornbread will soak up a great deal of the moisture). Spray a 9x13" baking dish with non-stick vegetable spray. Pour cornbread mixture into baking dish and place into the oven for forty minutes.

Tip: If the cornbread looks dry, you can pour additional remaining stock directly over the cornbread and it will readily soak it up.

Green Bean Bundles

For me, this was a game-changer recipe! I never would have thought to do a sweet sticky glaze over green beans before I learned this one. The sauce flavors are reminiscent of Japanese cooking. People will empty that dish in a moment.

Three 14.5 oz. cans whole green beans, drained

1 lb. bacon, cut in half

1 c. brown sugar

3 tbsp. soy sauce

1 tbsp. Worcestershire sauce

½ c. melted butter

1 tsp. garlic salt

Preheat the oven to 350 degrees Fahrenheit.

Spray a 9x13" baking dish with non-stick vegetable spray. Wrap seven green beans in a strip of bacon and place into dish. Continue with the rest of the green beans. In a medium mixing bowl, combine brown sugar, soy sauce, butter, and garlic salt. Pour evenly over bacon bundles and bake for forty-five minutes.

German Potato Salad

I'd never entertained the idea of a hot potato salad until my husband made this for me. This recipe quickly replaced my cold potato salad. It's my all-time favorite.

My husband came from a German family that loved to cook and eat. On our first date, he asked me, "Have you ever seen a picture of a ton of ants?" Well, that was a little odd, but I was game. "No," I said. He pulled out a family album with a picture of his five German aunts. None of them was under 300 pounds. They looked like they had intravenous kuchen every day! But man, could they cook! The men in Ron's family were all the size of a pencil, but they were fed!

2½ lb. small red potatoes, cut into quarters, unpeeled

1 large yellow onion, diced

1 lb. bacon, cut into half-inch pieces

One 10.5 oz. can cream of mushroom soup, undiluted

One 10.5 oz. can cream of celery soup, undiluted

3 tbsp. white vinegar

Salt and pepper to taste

In a large stock pot, place five quarts water and season with two teaspoon salt. Boil the potatoes until just tender, but still a little firm. Meanwhile, in a large skillet, cook bacon over medium heat, until crisp. Drain off excess fat, leaving about one tablespooon in the pan. Sauté the onions until translucent. Add soup and heat through. Add the vinegar, mix well, and taste to determine if more salt and pepper are needed. Return the bacon to the pan. Pour mixture over potatoes and mix well. Serve hot or chilled.

Cheesy Grits

Grits are one of those Southern foods that might be unfamiliar to you. People who think breakfast grits are too bland and boring usually still like grits when they're cooked with cheese.

3½ c. water

1 c. uncooked stone-ground grits

8 oz. sharp cheddar cheese, grated

4 oz. fire-roasted chilies, hot or mild

(optional)

¼ c. unsalted butter

Salt and pepper to taste

In a medium saucepan, bring three and a half cups of water to a boil over medium high heat. Whisk in grits and cook, whisking constantly, until they begin to thicken, about three minutes. Cover, reduce heat to low and cook, stirring occasionally until grits are tender and soft and cooked through, about fifteen minutes. When stirring, scrape the bottom of the pan to be sure that they don't stick and scorch. Remove from heat and stir in cheese, chilies and butter. Salt and pepper to taste and cover to keep warm.

Cheesy Grits Casserole

One recipe Cheesy Grits (above)

8 oz. cream cheese

2 eggs, beaten

1 tbsp. minced garlic

Preheat the oven to 375 degrees Fahrenheit.

You can easily turn Cheesy Grits into a casserole. Cook the grits as above and add the cheeses, chilies, plus the cream cheese, and garlic. Temper the eggs by stirring a small portion of the hot grits into them, stirring constantly so the eggs and grits will mix together instead of cooking the eggs. Gradually add the tempered eggs to the grits' mixture, a little portion at a time, until well-blended. Pour mixture into an 8x8" casserole dish that has been sprayed with non-stick spray. Bake for 35-40 minutes until golden on top. Allow to rest for 10-15 minutes so it will thicken for easy serving.

Variation: Another way to finish this dish for serving is to chill, slice into half-inch portions, and pan fry until crispy.

Creamy Roasted Garlic Mashed Potatoes

1 head garlic

1 tbsp. oil

2 lb. Yukon gold potatoes peeled and cut into two-inch cubes

One 8 oz. package Philadelphia cream cheese, cubed, and then softened

¼ c. tightly-packed fresh parsley, chopped

2 tbsp. milk

1½ tsp. Better than Bouillon, chicken flavor

Preheat the oven to 375 degrees Fahrenheit.

Cut off the top of the head of unpeeled garlic to expose the tops of the cloves. Place garlic, cut side up, on a sheet of foil and drizzle with oil. Wrap the foil around the garlic and place it in a small roasting pan. Roast for forty-five minutes. Cool slightly. In a large saucepan, while garlic is roasting, cook the potatoes in boiling water for about twenty minutes, until tender. Squeeze the roasted garlic from each clove into the potatoes, add cream cheese, parsley, milk, cubed butter, and bouillon. Using a hand mixer or masher combine to desired consistency.

Breads and Quick Breads

Everyone loves home-baked breads and quick breads. They're good as part of your everyday menu, and they're an especially good way to fill out a meal when you have unexpected guests.

The only miracle that all four Gospel writers tell us about (except for the resurrection itself) is the time Jesus managed to feed 5,000 people with just five loaves of bread and two fishes. (Matt. 14:13-21, Mark 6:31-44, Luke 9:12-17, and John 6:1-14). (Matt. 15:32-29, Mark 8:1-9). Making sure that everyone has enough to eat was important to Jesus, and it's important to me.

Your homemade breads can easily stretch a meal that wasn't planned for a crowd. And since everyone loves home-baked breads, your family and guests will be delighted.

Sourdough Bread

This recipe calls for sourdough starter. You can make your own sourdough starter or buy freeze-dried starter online. Some local bakeries might be willing to sell you starter by the cup.

To make your own starter, put equal parts flour and water in a mason jar and leave it open on the counter for ten days. That allows it to collect natural yeasts from the air. Stir it every day. The natural yeasts in the air will ferment it. If you add yeast or sugar, as some recipes do, you'll have to feed it. That makes the whole process more complicated, so I prefer this approach.

If you buy freeze-dried starter online, follow the instructions for reconstituting it and allowing it to ferment on your counter.

1 c. water

⅝ c. sourdough starter

⅛ c. olive oil

4 c. bread flour (such as King Arthur)

½ tbsp. salt

Preheat the oven to 450 degrees Fahrenheit.

Into a large bowl, add water, starter, and olive oil, mixing thoroughly. Add the flour and salt and mix with your hands until all flour is incorporated. This dough will look very rough. Cover the bowl with plastic or a damp kitchen towel and allow it to rest for thirty minutes to one hour (longer is better if you have the time). Allow to rest at room temperature to rise for the first time. Dough is ready when it is puffy and no longer looks dense. After thirty minutes, remove from bowl and do a few stretches by taking hold of the top of the dough and folding into the center. Turn the dough slightly and repeat. Continue until you have gone all the way around the loaf. If time is not an issue, return to the bowl for another thirty-minute rising time. Line the bottom of a Dutch oven with parchment paper. Place the dough in the Dutch oven for its second rise. Let rise for thirty minutes to one hour.

Just before the dough goes into the oven, slash a 2-3 cut on the top of the loaf with a paring knife or serrated blade. This allows for steam to escape and the dough to expand. Cover with the Dutch oven's lid and bake on the center oven rack for twenty minutes. Carefully remove the hot lid to reveal a shiny loaf. Continue to bake for an additional forty minutes until it turns into a deep, golden brown. Internal temperature should read 205–210 degrees Fahrenheit. Cool for at least one hour on a wire rack. Cutting into it before the hour is up will give it a gummy texture. If you want an even crispier crust, crack the oven door open for the last ten minutes to release the steam.

Sourdough Cinnamon Rolls

I would usually make this recipe for a weekend brunch.

Dough

⅔ c. milk

2 tbsp. butter, melted

1 large egg

½ c. starter

2 tbsp. granulated sugar

Two ½ c. all-purpose flour

Cinnamon Sugar Mixture

6 tbsp. butter, softened

½ c. granulated sugar

3 tsp. ground cinnamon

1 tbsp. flour

Glaze

2 tbsp. unsalted butter, softened

½ c. whipped cream cheese

¼–½ c. powdered sugar

1–2 tbsp. milk

The night before baking, make the dough. Combine the milk and butter in a small bowl. Into a stand mixer place the egg, starter, and sugar. Using the paddle attachment, mix to combine. While the mixer is running, slowly pour in the milk mixture. Add the flour and the salt. Continue to mix until a rough and sticky dough forms. Scrape down sides of mixing bowl, cover bowl with a damp towel and rest for thirty minutes. After resting, switch to the dough hook. Knead on medium low for 6-8 minutes. Dough should feel supple and readily pull away from the sides of the bowl. If it is sticky, add a small amount of flour. Spray a medium-sized bowl with cooking spray and transfer dough. Cover with plastic wrap and let rise. About thirty minutes into the rise, remove dough from bowl and stretch. Pull the top of the dough, stretching it, and then folding into the center of the dough. Turn slightly and repeat. Continue to turn and stretch until you have gone full circle. Return to bowl, cover with plastic wrap and let rise overnight, until doubled in size.

To bake, line a 9" springform pan with parchment paper on the bottom and the sides. The easiest way is to first ball the paper up and then spread it out across the bottom of the pan and up the sides. Spray your work surface lightly with cooking spray and then sprinkle with flour to prevent sticking. Remove dough from bowl and pat into a rough rectangle. Let rest for ten minutes. Dust the dough and rolling pin with flour and roll out into a 16x12" rectangle. It is helpful to measure with a tape. Make the cinnamon sugar mixture, using the cinnamon, sugar, and flour. Incorporate the softened butter with the sugar mix and spread over the dough, leaving a half-inch margin on all sides. Starting on the long side of the roll, roll into a log, pressing down. This needs to be a tight roll, so be patient. Mark the dough in 2" sections and cut with a bench scraper or oiled knife. Place into lined pan and let rise for 1-2 hours. Bake in a preheated oven at 350 degrees Fahrenheit for 35-40 minutes. Remove from oven and let cool in the pan for fifteen minutes, then lift out, using the parchment, and transfer to a wire rack. While the rolls are cooling, make the glaze. Place butter, cream cheese, and powered sugar into stand mixer. Beat smooth, thinning out with a little milk, if needed. Spread over top of rolls and serve.

Tip: You've seen internet cooks line a springform pan by precisely cutting parchment paper to cover the bottom of the pan and cutting a separate piece for the sides. That's fine for a delicate cake, but my simpler approach works well for these rolls.

Buttermilk Biscuits

In the South, biscuits are a big deal. When you go to any supermarket, you'll find racks and racks of different kinds of flour, because everyone wants to make their biscuits with the same brand their grandmother used. I never got that fussy. You don't have to be a princess about it to get great biscuits! As long as there's enough baking powder and baking soda, your biscuits are going to rise.

2 ⅔ c. all-purpose flour, plus more, for dusting

1½ tsp. baking powder

1½ tsp. baking soda

1 tsp. fine sea salt

2 tbsp. vegetable shortening, chilled

½ c. unsalted butter, frozen or very cold

One ⅓ c. chilled buttermilk

Preheat the oven to 450 degrees Fahrenheit.

Whisk together flour, baking powder, baking soda, and salt in a large bowl. Add the cold shortening, and working with a fork or a pastry blender, work the shortening into the flour mixture until the mixture resembles coarse cornmeal. Using the large holes of a box grater, grate the frozen butter and blend quickly with the flour-shortening mix until the butter pieces are well coated. Lightly spray a surface with vegetable spray and sprinkle with flour. Add buttermilk to the flour mixture in the bowl and stir together to form a sticky dough with no dry flour remaining. Turn dough out onto the floured surface. Coat your hands lightly with flour and gently pat the dough using the heels of your hands to form a ½"thick rectangle about 11x7". Fold rectangle into thirds. Repeat this process two more times, patting down the dough then folding into thirds. Using a floured 2½" cookie cutter, cut dough, pressing straight down, not twisting the cookie cutter. Reshape the scraps and continue to cut until all dough is used. Turn biscuits smooth side up an inch apart on a baking sheet. Refrigerate, uncovered, until cold, about fifteen minutes. Bake the chilled dough in the preheated oven for 16-20 minutes until the tops are golden brown.

Important! Yes, you really do need to avoid twisting that cutter when you cut your biscuits. If you twist the cutter, it will seal the edges of your biscuits so they won't rise properly. You'll get lovely high biscuit centers and flat little biscuit edges. No twisting!

Help! My biscuits still didn't rise! OK, now we're going to the expert advice arena. Biscuits rise best with a flour made from softer wheat, like Martha White or King Arthur All-Purpose Flour. But if those aren't available near you, try doubling the amounts of baking powder and baking soda to help a harder wheat flour rise properly.

Cornbread

Cornbread is a very galvanizing topic in the South! Do you make it sweet or not? (Southerners say: "Not!") Do you add things like corn, hot peppers, or cheese? I always add jalapeños, because I like it hot. I tend not to include cheese, because I often serve cornbread with chili, with cheese for topping.

2 c. self-rising cornmeal mix

2 eggs

2 tbsp. vegetable oil or melted bacon fat

One 4 oz. can diced, fire-roasted jalapeños (Optional: Omit or adjust quantity to your taste.)

¼ c. vegetable oil (if you're using cast iron)

1¾ c. buttermilk

Preheat the oven to 400 degrees Fahrenheit.

Preheat the oven to 400 degrees Fahrenheit.

If you're going to cook this in a 9" cast iron skillet, put the quarter cup vegetable oil in it and place in the hot oven while you make your batter. Put the cornmeal in a bowl and add the two tablespoon vegetable oil, the egg, and the buttermilk, plus the jalapeños if you're using them. Mix until thoroughly combined. Test the heat of the skillet by dropping a small amount of batter in the pan. It should sizzle. Pour the rest of the batter to an inch from the top of the skillet. Transfer to the hot oven and bake for 25-30 minutes until set and golden. If you are brave, flip the hot cornbread in the pan to display the crispy bottom.

Tip: If you are not using cast iron, omit the one-fourth cup vegetable oil. Spray an 8x8" baking dish with non-stick spray and do not preheat.

Hush Puppies

1½ c. cornmeal

½ c. flour

1½ tsp. salt

1 tsp. pepper

2 eggs

½ c. buttermilk

1 large diced yellow onion

One 4 oz. can diced green chilies (hot or mild as desired)

3 c. vegetable oil

In a deep pot, heat vegetable oil to 375 degrees Fahrenheit.

Mix together cornmeal, flour, salt, and pepper. In a separate bowl, mix together buttermilk and eggs, whisking to blend. Stir into dry mixture. Add onion and green chilies. Using a kitchen spoon or an ice cream scoop, drop balls of cornmeal into the oil and fry for three minutes or until browned on all sides. Serve immediately. Enjoy!

Serving Suggestion: These are great served as an accompaniment to any seafood. They go well with hot sauce, tartar sauce, or cocktail sauce.

Banana Bread

3 very overripe bananas

8 tbsp. butter, at room temperature

¾ c. granulated sugar

2 eggs, beaten lightly

1½ c. all-purpose flour

1 tsp. baking powder

½ tsp. salt

1 tsp. vanilla extract

1 c. chopped walnuts

Preheat the oven to 350 degrees Fahrenheit.

Spray a loaf pan with non-stick cooking spray and set aside. In a mixing bowl, on medium speed, cream together softened butter and sugar. Mash bananas with a fork or hand masher. Add the bananas and the eggs to the bowl, mixing batter thoroughly. In a separate bowl, mix the flour, baking soda, and salt. Slowly add to the batter, mixing thoroughly. Add vanilla extract and the walnuts. Pour into loaf pan and bake for 55-60 minutes, until a toothpick inserted in the center comes out clean. Remove from oven and rest for ten minutes, before transferring to a cooling rack to cool completely.

Tip: A banana is ready for banana bread when the skin is brown all over.

Candies

Candies, like cookies, make wonderful holiday or hostess gifts. They're also great to bring into work to share with coworkers. Gifting and sharing are great practices, if for no other reason, than you probably don't want to keep the whole batch in your house! Otherwise, you might be as tempted as I am to eat an entire batch in a couple of days.

English Butter Toffee

This is a rich, buttery toffee that makes for a beautiful and tasty gift. When I take it to work, they rave over it! It's very easy to make. I like to finish it by sprinkling with Maldon sea salt. That salt makes a beautiful presentation with its great big pyramid-shaped crystals. If you can't get it where you live, you can order it online as I do.

Two 12 oz. bags of chocolate or dark chocolate chips

2 c. butter

2 c. granulated sugar

2 c. almonds, roughly-chopped, then divided

Large crystal sea salt (optional)

Cover a cookie sheet with either aluminum foil or parchment paper. Melt one twelve-ounce bag of chocolate chips in the microwave in thirty-second increments until liquid. Pour onto the covered cookie sheet, spread evenly, and place in freezer.

Place butter and sugar into a large heavy-bottomed pot. Using over medium heat to 285 degrees Fahrenheit, stir occasionally. (Use a candy thermometer to monitor the temperature.) Remove from heat and stir in one and a half cups of almonds. Pulse the remaining almonds in a food processor until they form a dust. Take the cookie sheet out of the freezer. Pour the still warm toffee-almond mixture over the cooled chocolate and spread it evenly. Pour the remaining twelve ounces of chocolate chips over the toffee. When the heat of the toffee has melted them, spread evenly, and dust the top with the pulsed almond powder. If you use the sea salt, sprinkle this over the top to finish.

Tip: If sugar crystals are forming on the sides of the pan, do not scrape the crystals into the mixture. Just wipe the side of the pan above the crystals with a wet pastry brush. That will dissolve the crystals and wash them back into the cooking mixture.

Cracker Crack

There is no better name for this saltine cracker toffee than crack because it's so addictive! I have also heard it referred to as Christmas Crack, but it's so easy you may as well make a batch any time of year.

40-50 saltine crackers (salted tops)

1 c. salted butter, cubed

1 c. light brown sugar, packed

1 tsp. vanilla

2 c. chocolate chips (milk, semi-sweet, or dark)

1 c. chopped and toasted pecans or M&Ms candies (optional)

Preheat the oven to 375 degrees Fahrenheit.

Line a baking sheet with aluminum foil and spray with non-stick cooking spray. Spread the crackers in one even layer on the baking sheet. In a medium saucepan, over medium heat, combine the butter and the brown sugar. Once the butter has melted and begun to combine with the brown sugar, stir with a wooden spoon until the mixture starts to bubble. Set a timer for three minutes and allow it to continue to boil. Pour evenly over the saltines and place in the oven for five minutes. Remove from the oven and immediately sprinkle the chocolate chips over the surface. Let set for 2-3 minutes until the chips have begun to soften, and then spread evenly with a spatula. If using, sprinkle pecans and/or M&M's over the top. Let cool for two hours at room temperature or you can speed this process up by placing in the refrigerator or the freezer. When completely cooled, break apart and store in an airtight tin.

60-Second Fudge

This is truly a sixty-second fudge that makes a great hostess or holiday gift.

One 12 oz. package chocolate chips

One 14 oz. can sweetened condensed milk

In a microwave safe bowl, pour sweetened condensed milk over chocolate chips. Cook in the microwave on high heat for one minute. Remove from the microwave and stir until smooth. Add nuts, if using. Pour into an 8x8" buttered baking dish. Chill for thirty minutes and add toppings, pressing down lightly into surface.

Variations: There are many things you can do to change this up and add variety. For example, you could add one cup of any of your favorite nuts, roughly chopped. You can also top it with crushed peppermint candies or pretzels for a sweet and salty treat.

Quick and Easy Turtles

It doesn't matter how many you make, these will disappear very quickly!

1 bag mini pretzel twists

One 34.5 oz. party-sized bag Rolo candies

Pecan halves

Preheat the oven to 300 degrees Fahrenheit.

Spray a cookie sheet with non-stick vegetable spray and lay pretzels out in a single layer. Top each pretzel twist with one Rolo candy. Place it into the oven and turn off the heat. After five minutes, remove the cookie sheet from the oven, and smash down each candy with pecan half. Let cool.

Peanut Brittle

2 c. sugar

1 c. light corn syrup

½ c. water

2 c. roasted salted peanuts

2 tbsp. butter

1½ tsp. baking soda

1½ tsp. vanilla

This is a recipe that requires a candy thermometer. Line a sheet pan with parchment paper and set aside. Measure peanuts, butter, baking soda, and vanilla, and set aside, each in its own bowl or other container. This makes it easy to add them quickly to the hot sugar syrup later. In a medium saucepan or a medium cast-iron skillet, stir together the sugar and water. Add the corn syrup and stir well. Cook over medium heat until the mixture comes to a gentle boil. Be patient and don't turn the heat up! Cook, stirring occasionally until the mixture comes to 250 degrees. Add the peanuts, and stirring constantly, heat the mixture to 300 degrees. Add the butter, baking soda and vanilla to the pan, stirring thoroughly. Pour out mixture onto the prepared cookie sheet, spread it into a single layer, and allow it to cool.

The Why behind the recipe: The baking soda will cause the brittle to foam into a kind of honeycomb. This is necessary so that the brittle will not be too hard to bite into.

Cookies

Cookies are one of those early cooking projects that are so satisfying to do with children. Even if you're slicing them off a roll of refrigerated cookie dough from the store, a five-year-old will love to watch through the oven door as they brown. Be sure to turn the oven light on for them! When you take the cookies out, they'll be so proud to say, "Look what we did!"

I am so grateful to have lived in a way that allowed me to learn what I've learned, and to pass it on to my children and other people's children.

Chocolate Chip Cookies

My son's best friend since the fifth grade always wanted to come to our house because he knew I would be cooking. Some days I would walk into the kitchen and discover that he and my son had gone to the store and bought all the ingredients for chocolate chip cookies. They would leave the ingredients on the counter with a note that said, "You know what to do."

2½ c. all-purpose flour

1 tsp. baking soda

1 tsp. salt

1 c. vegetable shortening

¼ c. water

¾ c. granulated sugar

¾ c. packed brown sugar

1 tsp. vanilla extract

2 large eggs

One 12-oz. package chocolate chips

1 c. chopped nuts (optional)

Whisk together flour, baking soda, and salt in a small bowl, and set aside. In a large mixing bowl, beat vegetable shortening, water, granulated sugar, brown sugar, and vanilla extract. Add eggs, one at a time, mixing thoroughly between editions. Beat in the chocolate chips and nuts, if using. Drop by rounded spoonsful onto a cookie sheet that has either been sprayed with non-stick spray or covered in parchment paper. Bake for 9-11 minutes, or until golden brown. Remove from oven and place cookies onto a baking rack to cool.

Easy Substitutions: If you don't have brown sugar, substitute white sugar (three-fourth cup minus one tablespoon) and add one tablespoon of molasses.

Peanut Butter Cookies

⅔ c. creamy peanut butter

½ c. shortening

½ c. sugar

½ c. firmly-packed brown sugar

1 large egg

2 tbsp. milk

1 tsp. vanilla extract

1½ c. all-purpose flour

1 tsp. baking soda

¼ tsp. salt

Preheat the oven to 350 degrees Fahrenheit.

In a small bowl, combine flour, baking soda, and salt. Whisk together until well-blended and set aside. In a large mixing bowl, cream together peanut butter, shortening, sugar, egg, milk, and vanilla at high speed until well-blended and fluffy. Add the flour mixture and mix just until blended. With your hands, make one and a half-inch balls of the mixture, place them on the cookie sheet, and flatten with a fork in a crisscross pattern. Bake for 8-9 minutes until golden brown on the edges. Remove cookie sheet from oven and allow cookies to rest for two minutes. Place cookies on a wire rack to cool completely.

Sugar Cookies

2 ¾ c. all-purpose flour

1 tsp. baking soda

½ tsp. baking powder

1 c. vegetable shortening plus 3 tbsp. water

1½ c. granulated sugar

1 large egg

1 tsp. vanilla extract

Preheat the oven to 350 degrees Fahrenheit.

In a small bowl, stir flour, baking soda, and baking powder together, and set aside. In a large mixing bowl, blend together the sugar and the shortening and water until smooth and creamy. Add the egg and the vanilla extract, combining well. Gradually add the flour mixture. With your hands, roll into walnut-sized balls and place on greased cookie sheet two inches apart. Bake 8-10 minutes until the edges are golden. Remove from the oven and allow the cookies to rest for two minutes on the pan before using a spatula to move them to a wire rack to cool completely.

Tip: The easiest way to grease your cookie sheet is to spray it with non-stick vegetable pan spray.

Easy Variations: Dip the balls of cookie dough in sugar or chopped nuts. Place them on the cookie sheet with the dipped side up.

No-bake Haystack Cookies

1⅔ c. sugar

½ c. milk

½ c. butter

¼ tsp. salt

½ c. unsweetened cocoa powder

½ tsp. vanilla extract

3 c. quick cooking oats

1 c. unsweetened coconut

Prepare a cookie sheet by either spraying it with non-stick spray or covering it with parchment paper.

In a medium saucepan, over medium heat, mix the sugar, milk, butter, and salt. When the mixture just begins to boil, add the cocoa powder and continue to cook, stirring constantly, for four minutes. If the mixture begins to look too dry, you can add milk a few drops at a time. Add the oats and the coconut at once and stir well to blend. This will set up very quickly so working fast, drop by spoonfuls onto the prepared cookie sheet.

Cakes and Cheesecakes

My grandmother always had some kind of cake in the house, but I think of them as something to celebrate an occasion: a birthday, an anniversary, a graduation. They're not everyday cooking. There has to be a reason to make them. And cheesecakes are special! They're richer, so they need less adornment. I love a plain cheesecake more than I love one with toppings. But that's just me. . .You should make cakes and cheesecakes whenever you want and however you like!

Sourdough Carrot Cake

This cake has been a family favorite since the seventies, when I made it for my son's third birthday. He loved it, and I've made it for his birthday ever since. When he was in Iraq, I'd vacuum-seal it and freeze it and send it there. He had his birthday every year he was deployed. This recipe uses sourdough starter for moisture, meaning that you don't need to add applesauce or raisins or any other additives to keep it moist. If it lasts a week—which is not likely—it will be as fresh as the day it came out of the oven. You can buy starter online and sometimes your local bakery will sell you starter by the cup. You can also make your own starter. . .see the directions in the recipe for Sourdough Bread above. Just a heads up: Making your own starter takes ten days, so plan ahead!

2 c. all-purpose flour

2 c. granulated sugar

1 tsp. salt

1 tsp. baking soda

1 tsp. baking powder

1 tsp. cinnamon

4 eggs

1 c. sourdough starter

1 c. vegetable oil

2 c. grated carrot

Preheat the oven to 350 degrees Fahrenheit.

Mix dry ingredients thoroughly in a large mixing bowl. Add eggs, sourdough starter, oil, and grated carrots to dry ingredients. Stir until moistened, then mix on medium speed of mixer for two minutes. Pour into a 9x13" baking dish that has been sprayed with non-stick vegetable spray. Tap the pan against the countertop to get out any bubbles. Bake it at 350 degrees Fahrenheit for fifty-five minutes. Remove from oven and place on cooling rack. Cool completely and frost with cream cheese frosting.

Cream Cheese Frosting

16 oz. cream cheese

1 stick butter

3 c. powdered sugar

1½ tsp. vanilla extract

Soften cream cheese and butter to room temperature. In a large mixing bowl, thoroughly cream them together at medium speed. Lower the speed and gradually add the powdered sugar, blending a little at a time. When all the sugar is incorporated and the frosting is smooth, remove from the mixer, and stir in the vanilla extract.

Chocolate Roll

Okay, this really feels like cheating. This is the fastest, easiest dessert you have ever made. I suspect it probably started during the Depression. Or maybe it was invented by someone who was craving chocolate (a woman with PMS?), but lived too far from town to drive in, just to buy a candy bar. This makes two flat-folded chocolate-filled treats that no one will be able to stop eating until they're all gone. It is fast, easy, and will disappear in no time!

2 store-bought or homemade pie crusts

1 c. granulated sugar

3 tbsp. unsweetened cocoa powder

2 sticks cold butter

Preheat the oven to 400 degrees Fahrenheit.

Use homemade pie crust or roll out the kind of crust you buy from the dairy case. Don't judge: We're making emergency chocolate here! Roll out pie crust. In a small bowl, mix sugar and cocoa powder until well-combined. Sprinkle over each pie crust to within one inch of the edges. Cut butter into half-inch cubes and dot all over the surface of the chocolate sugar. Fold up into thirds and tuck the ends underneath to seal each crust, giving you two long, flat rolls. Place on a baking sheet, sprayed with non-stick spray. Bake for thirty minutes, until golden brown and crusty. Try to be patient until it's cool enough to slice and eat. You can do some serious damage to your mouth if you jump in too soon!

Tip: If you want to use a homemade pie crust, I've included a recipe in the Pies and Cobblers section.

Cheesecake

This is another recipe that seems to be without limit as to how you can change it up. (Just look at the case at the front of the Cheesecake Factory!) I am giving you the basics, but also giving you license to go any direction you prefer.

Crust

2 c. crushed graham crackers

⅓ c. unsalted melted butter

⅓ c. sugar

Melt butter and pour into a small bowl. Add the crushed crackers and stir with a fork to moisten and combine. Spray an 8" springform pan with cooking spray. Pour the mixture into the pan, flatten evenly all over the bottom, and one inch up the sides. Using the bottom of a glass to flatten the crust helps get the crust well-packed and even. Place in the refrigerator until the filling is ready.

Filling

Two 8 oz. blocks cream cheese, softened

3 eggs

1 c. sugar

16 oz. sour cream

1 lemon, zested

1 tsp. vanilla extract

Preheat the oven to 325 degrees Fahrenheit.

You need a springform baking pan. With an electric mixer on low speed, beat the cream cheese until smooth and with no lumps. Add the eggs, one at a time, and continue to combine thoroughly. Slowly add the sugar and beat 1-2 minutes until creamy. Add the sour cream, lemon zest, and vanilla extract. Scrape down the sides of the bowl periodically. Take the crust-lined pan out of the refrigerator. Pour the smooth mixture into the prepared pan and smooth the top. Place a large sheet of aluminum foil around the bottom and sides of the pan to seal it from the water bath that you will use. Place the cake pan into a large roasting pan and fill halfway up the cake pan with boiling water. This will keep the cake from cracking as it cooks. Bake for forty-five minutes—center will seem to be not quite set but will firm up as it chills. Remove from water bath and let rest for thirty minutes at room temperature. Chill in refrigerator for at least four hours. To unmold, run a thin metal spatula around the inside rim. Release springform and unmold. Slice with a thin, sharp knife that has been dipped in warm water. Clean knife after each cut.

Tip: The easy way to crush graham crackers or other cookies is to place them in a plastic bag, set the bag on your counter, then roll over it with your rolling pin (or a bottle) until the crumbs are the size you want. Pour them into your measuring cup. If you find you haven't made enough, just roll some more. If you have extra, set them aside to sprinkle on top of a cake or pudding.

No-Bake Cheesecake

This recipe is for occasions when you need a dessert but are totally strapped for time. You can make the filling and the crust, or you can buy store-bought premade crust, and even buy the filling by the tub in the dairy case! This recipe uses a store-bought crust and whipped topping but you will make the filling yourself. You can dress this up with any toppings you choose such as fresh fruit or canned pie filling.

Filling

One 8 oz. package cream cheese, softened

1 c. sour cream

½ c. sugar

2 tsp. vanilla extract

One 8 oz. container Cool Whip, thawed 4 hrs. in refrigerator

One precooked pie crust (usually a graham cracker or cookie crust for this recipe)

⅓ c. melted butter

⅓ c. sugar

Melt butter and pour into a small bowl. Add the crushed crackers and sugar and stir with a fork to moisten and combine. Spray an 8" springform pan with cooking spray. Pour the mixture into the pan and flatten evenly all over the bottom and one inch up the sides. Using the bottom of a glass to flatten the crust helps get the crust well-packed and even. Place in the refrigerator until the filling is ready.

Avocado Key Lime "Pie"

I know what you're thinkin. . .WHAT!?! I didn't want to love it, either, but I had never liked the texture of key lime pie. I'm not a custardy kind of gal. This pie is more like a cheesecake in texture to me, which I'm ALL about. You won't even know the avocado is there! So, c'mon! Take a chance. Just like with anything you make, if you hate it, you don't have to ever make it again. (But I dare you to hate it!)

Crust

1 sleeve graham crackers, finely-crushed

⅓ c. sugar

⅓ c. butter, melted

Spray an 8" springform pan or pie plate with non-stick spray.

In a medium bowl, mix crackers and sugar. Pour butter evenly over top and stir with a fork to moisten all crumbs. Press into pie plate, using the bottom of a drinking glass, covering the bottom and sides. Refrigerate while you make the filling.

Filling

2 large, firm, but ripe avocados, pitted and peeled

2 tsp. lime zest

2 tsp. lemon zest

¾ c. key lime juice

One 14 oz. can sweetened condensed milk

1½ tsp. vanilla extract

Using an electric mixer, beat avocados on medium speed until smooth and creamy, scraping down sides of bowl as necessary. Add lime zest, lemon zest, and key lime juice, beating to incorporate. Add sweetened condensed milk and vanilla, and continue to beat until very smooth. Pour into prepared crust and cover with plastic, pressing down to remove all bubbles. Freeze for at least four hours. Ten minutes before serving, remove from freezer and allow to thaw slightly. Garnish with lime zest or key lime slices. Add whipped cream if desired.

Pies and Cobblers

Who doesn't have a favorite pie? Whether you think apple, peach, cherry, chocolate, or pumpkin pie rules, we haven't even scratched the surface of the universe of pies. Time for admission—we all have that one mountain that we just can't seem to climb. Mine is pie crust. I can make it ten times the same way and it will be different every time. Just never mastered it. But, no worries! The saving grace is that you can BUY pie crust already made! The freezer and the dairy section of the supermarket both have pie crust. One is frozen, comes in a pan, and needs to be thawed completely so it won't crack. The other comes in a box or tube and you want to let it warm to room temperature so it softens before you roll it out. Magic AND time-saving!!! I'm adding a recipe for pie crust, just in case you want to make your own. You can also make a cobbler, which has the same kind of yummy fruit filling, but makes its own soft, cake-like upper crust.

Basic Pie Crust

2½ c. all-purpose flour

1 tsp. kosher salt

6 tbsp. cold unsalted butter

¾ c. vegetable shortening, chilled

½ c. ice water

Mix flour and salt in a large mixing bowl. Add ice cubes to a measuring cup and fill to one-half-cup water and set aside. Add butter and chilled shortening and blend with two forks or a pastry blender until the mixture resembles small peas. Add ice water one tablespoon at a time, mixing it in with a fork until the dough forms. Be careful not to overwork the dough: that makes for tough pie crust. Continue to add ice water until a ball forms, divide it into two, and press into discs. Wrap well in plastic wrap and refrigerate for at least two hours and up to twenty-four. Roll out into rounds. This makes two crusts.

Tip: It's much easier to roll out pie crusts between two sheets of plastic wrap or waxed paper. That also lets you avoid adding extra flour while rolling, which can toughen the crust.

Tip: To cover the edges of a pie crust to prevent overbrowning, you can use three-inch strips of aluminum foil folded over the edges and pressed carefully into place. Some people find the easiest way to do this is to cut a sheet of foil in a circle. The outer edge of the foil circle is cut one-inch larger than your pie pan while the inner edge is cut about one and a half-inches smaller than your pan. So if you are using a 9" pie pan, you will cut a ten-inch circle of foil, then cut a seven and a half-inch circle out of the center of the foil. That gives you a hollow circle you can lay on top of the pie and gently fold over the outer edge of the pan to prevent the crimped edges of the crust from getting too brown. If you end up baking pies frequently, you can purchase a pie shield. I've used them, but when I started traveling I gave them away. Now I just use foil.

Apple Pie

An all-American dessert, apple pie can be made with any firm, tart apple. We prefer Granny Smith apples, but you can use Honeycrisp, Rome, Golden Delicious, Jonathan, Braeburn, or Northern Spy. All these varieties are crisp and tart and hold their shape well in the oven.

6 c. thinly-sliced peeled apples

¾ c. sugar

2 tbsp. all-purpose flour

¾ tsp. cinnamon

¼ tsp. salt

⅛ tsp. ground nutmeg

1 tbsp. lemon juice

Preheat the oven to 425 degrees Fahrenheit.

In a large bowl, mix apples, sugar, flour, cinnamon, salt, and nutmeg. Gently fold all ingredients together, then pour into a 9" pie pan. Sprinkle with the lemon juice and then cover with top crust. Turn edges of top crust under the base pie crust and pinch them together to crimp. With a small knife, cut three or four vent holes on the top. Bake for 40-45 minutes until the top is browned. After twenty minutes, if desired, you can cover the edges with three-inch-wide aluminum foil strips to keep them from over browning. Cool on a cookie rack for at least two hours before serving.

Peach Pie

1 box refrigerated pie crust	1–2 tsp. fresh minced ginger (optional)
3 lb. peaches	2 tbsp. cold unsalted butter
⅔ c. granulated sugar	1 large egg
½ c. all-purpose flour	1 tbsp. milk
1 tbsp. fresh lemon juice	1½ tbsp. Turbinado sugar (if desired)

Preheat the oven to 450 degrees Fahrenheit.

Unroll room temperature bottom crust and place into a 9" pie pan. Peel peaches and cut into chunks, not slices, preferably one-inch chunks. In a large bowl, mix peaches, sugar, flour, lemon, and ginger until well-mixed. Turn out into pie plate and even out. Cut the butter into small cubes and dot over surface. Place top crust, turning it under the edge of the bottom crust, and crimping it. Mix egg and milk and brush over top. If desired, sprinkle sugar over the top. Bake at 425 degrees for twenty minutes, then keeping the pie in the oven, lower temperature to 375 degrees. At this point, you can cover the outside edges with foil or a pie shield to avoid over-browning. Continue baking for 45–50 minutes. If center is becoming too brown, you may also place a round sheet of foil in the center. Cool for at least two hours before slicing to allow center to set up.

Variation: To make it "fancy," this pie is perfect for a latticed top crust. To make a lattice crust, cut top crust into strips and weave strips over and under each other, leaving small open panes. Serve with vanilla bean ice cream, if desired.

Cherry Pie

1 box refrigerated pie crust, room temperature

4½ c. pitted cherries, halved and quartered

⅔ c. granulated sugar

¼ c. cornstarch

1 tbsp. lemon juice

1 tsp. vanilla extract

¼ tsp. almond extract

1 tbsp. cold unsalted butter

1 large egg

1 tbsp. milk

Turbinado sugar or Sugar in the Raw

In a large bowl, stir together cherries, sugar, cornstarch, lemon juice, vanilla, and almond extracts. Place the bottom crust in the pie pan and press it gently into place. Using a slotted spoon, spoon cherry mixture into pie crust. Reserve the juice and place the pie in the refrigerator while you reduce the juice. To do this, put the remaining juice into a small saucepan. Over low heat, cook, stirring for about 4-5 minutes. Pour over the cherries in the pie plate and mix very gently. The juices will redistribute throughout the pie as it bakes. Cover with remaining crust and, if using a full top crust, make a few small knife slits to vent. Bake for twenty minutes, then, keeping pie in the oven, lower the heat to 375 degrees, and continue to bake for 30-40 minutes until crust is browned. (After twenty minutes, cover the outer edges of the crust to prevent over-browning. See tip below.) Remove from oven and cool for at least two hours. As with all fruit pies, if sliced warm, filling will not be set and juices will be runny.

Variations: You could use this recipe with any berry—blueberries, blackberries, raspberries, or others. If you cannot find fresh cherries, you may substitute cans cherry pie filling.

Traditional Key Lime Pie

Crust

1 sleeve graham crackers, finely-crushed

⅓ c. butter

⅓ c. butter, melted

In a medium bowl, combine crackers and sugar until well-blended. Pour butter evenly over surface and stir with a fork until all crumbs are moistened. Press into a 9" pie pan and cover bottom and sides evenly. (It helps to use the bottom of a drinking glass.) Refrigerate while you make the filling.

Filling

3 egg yolks

2 tsp. lime zest

One 14 oz. can sweetened condensed milk

⅔ c. key lime juice (freshly-squeezed or bottled)

In an electric mixer (wire whisk attachment if you have one), on high-speed, mix egg yolks and lime zest until very fluffy, about five minutes. Slowly incorporate the sweetened condensed milk and beat until thick, about 3-4 minutes. Lower the mixer speed to low and add lime juice, mixing until just blended, no longer. Bake for ten minutes until just set. Cool on a wire rack then refrigerate. Place in freezer for 10-20 minutes, just before serving. Top with lime zest and whipped cream, if desired.

Heads up! The difference between a lime and a key lime is that key limes are about the size of a quarter, so you need to devote a lot of time if you're squeezing them yourself. The best bottled key lime juice I've ever found is Nellie and Joe's Famous Key West Lime Juice. If you can get that, you'll love the results.

Fruit Cobbler

The main difference between pie and cobbler, as I see it, is that pies need to be cooled to prevent the juices from making the lower crust soggy. Cobblers are typically served warm and spooned out into bowls. With either one, you can't go wrong with the addition of a scoop of vanilla bean ice cream! Cobblers are usually made in a rectangular baking dish. A Midwestern cobbler has a crust top and bottom and takes a bit more work than this one. This cobbler makes its own crust on top only, and comes together super fast.

Filling

4 c. of desired fruit (see Note below)

¾ c. granulated sugar

¼ tsp. salt

Batter

6 tbsp. butter, melted

1 c. all-purpose flour

1 c. granulated sugar

2 tsp. baking powder

¼ tsp. salt

¾ c. milk

Preheat the oven to 350 degrees Fahrenheit.

Pour the melted butter into the bottom of a 9x13" baking dish. Mix together flour, sugar, baking powder, and salt. Add milk and stir until smooth. Pour over butter. Place fruit, sugar, and salt into medium saucepan and cook over medium heat for five minutes. Pour directly over batter. Do not stir! Bake for 38-40 minutes until crust has formed and is browned. Serve warm. Don't forget the ice cream!

Note: Favorite fruits for cobbler include blueberries, blackberries, cherries, apples, and peaches. You can make a cobbler with just one fruit or mix them. When you're using a fruit that has a core or stone, remove the core or stone and slice the fruit. I peel the fruit for my cobblers, but you don't have to.

Appetizers and Party Snacks

You can't have a cookbook without a list of easy, quick appetizers. They're the hit of every party! Although there are hundreds of great options, we will offer about twenty tried and true recipes for appetizers, party snacks, and, in the next section, crackers and dips. These have all been tried and proven to be crowd favorites that disappear quickly.

241

Baked Brie en Croute

No appetizer is more versatile than a baked brie. You can make it sweet or savory, and either way, it will be the first dish demolished at your party! I will give you the basic treatment and then offer variations. The seafood version is something I had for the first time at an event when my late husband was singing with the Denver Symphony. He was singing bass with the symphony while at the same time, I was singing country in the Marlboro 100. Then we had kids who were headbangers. We were all musical, but in totally different styles.

1 package frozen puff pastry, thawed

1 wheel brie cheese

1 egg

1 tbsp. water

Roll the puff pastry out in to two twelve-inch squares. Place the wheel of brie on one square and place the other square on top of the cheese, pressing down to make a seal. With a pizza cutter or a sharp knife, trim the pastry to one inch around the edge. Press with a fork to seal. Do not discard the remaining pastry since you can use it to make decorations for the top of the brie (see Tip below). Beat the egg and water together and brush this egg wash over the crust. If you are adding decorations, do that now—the egg wash will hold them in place—and then brush the decorations with egg wash to create a shiny glaze. Bake for twenty-five minutes and allow to rest for a minimum of ten minutes after removing from the oven.

Tip: To decorate the top of the brie, use cookie cutters to cut desired shapes, or cut freehand with a knife if you're confident! You can arrange overlapping triangles of puff pastry in a circle, place leaf cutouts for an autumn party, or anything you would like.

Variations: This is where you get creative! To make a sweet version, put toasted pecans and a drizzle of honey on top before adding top crust. Serve as above. To make a savory version, pour a can of Bookbinder's seafood bisque over the top of the cheese before you add the top crust.

Serve with

Sliced and toasted baguettes

Sliced granny Smith apples

Sliced pears

Red and green grapes

There are no limits to the ways you can serve this cheese. Serve with your choice of sliced fruit and toasty bread. It is a rich cheese, so tart fruits help balance out the richness.

Mini Potato Skins

1½ lb. Baby Dutch Yellow potatoes (about 20 2-inch potatoes)

1 tbsp. olive oil

4 oz. freshly-shredded sharp cheddar cheese

6 bacon slices, cooked and crumbled

½ c. sour cream

2 tbsp. finely-chopped chives

Preheat the oven to 425 degrees Fahrenheit.

Wash the potatoes and pat to dry. In a large bowl, toss the potatoes with the olive oil to thoroughly coat. Place on a baking sheet lined with parchment paper. Bake until tender, 17-20 minutes. Cool potatoes completely on the baking sheet. Slice potatoes in half and scoop out the flesh, leaving a one eight-inch shell. Reserve the flesh for another use. Turn the oven up to 450 degrees. Place potatoes, hollow side down on baking sheet. Cook for ten minutes, then turn over and cook 8-10 minutes more, until crisp. Fill potatoes with cheddar cheese and top with bacon crumbles. Bake at 450 degrees until cheese melts. Top with sour cream and chives.

Ham Cheese Ball

8 oz. cream cheese, softened

4 oz. smoked deli ham, finely-chopped

1½ oz. cheddar cheese, finely-grated

2 tbsp. finely-chopped scallion

2 tbsp. fresh flat leaf parsley, finely-chopped

2 tsp. onion powder

1 tsp. garlic powder

1 tsp. Dijon mustard

½ tsp. Worcestershire sauce

5 tbsp. finely-chopped chives, divided

½ c. toasted finely-chopped pecans

In a large bowl, stir together cream cheese, ham, cheddar, scallion, parsley, onion powder, garlic powder, Dijon, Worcestershire, and two tablespoons of chives until well-combined. Cover the bowl with plastic wrap and chill in the refrigerator for thirty minutes. Combine pecans and remaining chives in a shallow dish. Form the cheese mixture into a ball and roll it in the pecans and chives. Wrap in plastic wrap and refrigerate until firm, at least one hour or up to two days. Serve with buttery crackers.

Sausage Balls

3 c. baking mix, such as Bisquick

1 lb. pork sausage (I prefer hot)

16 oz. grated sharp cheddar cheese

½ c. milk

1 tsp. salt

1 tsp. freshly-ground black pepper

Preheat the oven to 350 degrees Fahrenheit.

Spray a rimmed cookie sheet with non-stick spray. In a large bowl, thoroughly combine all ingredients and shape into one-inch balls. Bake until brown, about 20-25 minutes. Best served warm.

Little Smokies

Another no-brainer use for your crockpot. Nothing is easier than this!

28 oz. Little Smokies (or other cocktail sausages)

1½ c. barbecue sauce (your choice)

½ c. light brown sugar

1 tsp. Worcestershire sauce

In the bottom of the slow cooker, stir together barbecue sauce, sugar and Worcestershire sauce. Add little smokies and stir to coat. Cover and cook on low for 2-3 hours. Lower temperature to warm to serve.

Deviled Eggs

12 whole hard-boiled eggs

½ c. mayonnaise

2 tbsp. yellow mustard

2 tsp. dill pickle juice

¼ tsp. kosher salt

¼ tsp. freshly-ground black pepper

dash hot sauce, if desired

paprika for sprinkling

chives, finely-chopped

For no-fail hard-boil eggs, put in a pot large enough that they fit in one layer. Cover them with water and bring to a boil. Then turn off heat, cover the pan, and allow to sit for twelve minutes. Immediately place into an ice-water bath so they cool instead of continuing to cook. Let stand for 5-10 minutes. Peel the eggs by draining the pot then gently shaking it. That will knock most of the eggshells off— less work for you! Clean the rest of the shells off under running water. When the shells are completely off the eggs, cut each egg in half. Scoop the yellow centers into a bowl. Mash with a fork until they are broken up. Add the mayonnaise, mustard, pickle juice, salt, pepper, and hot sauce, if desired. Stir together. Mixture should be mostly smooth. Spoon or pipe the filling back into the centers of the eggs. Sprinkle with paprika and refrigerate in an airtight container until ready to serve. Garnish with chives.

Variations: Add one and a half teaspoons of horseradish or hot sauce.

Pigs in a Blanket

1 package Little Smokies (cocktail sausages)

Two 8 oz. packages crescent rolls

Unroll crescent roll sheets to reveal eight triangles. Cut each one into three triangles. Put one little smoky on the wide end of a triangle and roll up to the point. On a baking sheet, place it point side down. Repeat with remaining sausages. Bake for 9-10 minutes until golden brown.

Almond Bacon Cheese Crostini

1 baguette, cut into 36 diagonal slices

2 c. shredded Monterey jack cheese

⅔ c. mayonnaise

½ c. sliced almonds, toasted

6 slices bacon, cooked and crumbled

1 green onion, chopped

Dash salt

Preheat the oven to 400 degrees Fahrenheit.

Place bread slices on an ungreased cookie sheet. Bake for 8-9 minutes, until golden brown.

Meanwhile, in a large bowl, combine cheese, mayonnaise, almonds, bacon, and onion. Spread on bread slices. Bake until cheese is melted, 7-8 minutes.

Ham Sliders

2 tbsp. mayonnaise

2 tsp. Dijon mustard

½ tsp. flaky sea salt (such as Maldon), divided

One 12 oz. package Hawaiian dinner rolls (such as King's Hawaiian)

12 deli ham slices (8 oz.)

6 slices gouda cheese (4 oz.)

1 tbsp. unsalted butter, melted

2 tsp. "Everything" bagel seasoning

Preheat the oven to 375 degrees Fahrenheit.

Spray a baking sheet with non-stick spray and set aside. Stir together the mayonnaise, mustard, and one-fourth teaspoon of salt. Do not separate the rolls: Cut them horizontally all at once with a long, serrated knife. Spread the mayonnaise mixture on both cut sides of the rolls. Fold ham slices and place ham and cheese on top of rolls. Replace top rolls. Brush butter evenly over tops of rolls and sprinkle with the remaining salt and "Everything" bagel seasoning. Place on baking sheet and cover with aluminum foil. Bake for eight minutes. Remove foil and bake seven minutes more. Separate and serve immediately.

Variation: If you live in the South, you're more familiar with ham biscuits. They're almost exactly the same. Just substitute your own baked buttermilk biscuits (see recipe in the Breads and Quick Breads section) for the Hawaiian rolls and omit the bagel seasoning.

Savory Spiced Pecans

4 c. pecan halves

⅓ c. unsalted butter, melted

2 tsp. Worcestershire sauce

1¼ tsp. kosher salt

½ tsp. garlic powder

½ tsp. mustard powder

¼ tsp. cayenne pepper

½ tsp. Tabasco sauce

Preheat the oven to 300 degrees Fahrenheit.

Place pecans into a large bowl. In a second bowl, mix all other ingredients. Drizzle over pecan halves and stir to coat the pecans. Arrange pecans in a single layer on a large baking sheet. Bake for 20-22 minutes, stirring halfway into cooking time. Cool completely, stirring occasionally. Store in an airtight container.

Chex Party Mix

There's a reason this snack has been on the table since the recipe was first introduced more than sixty years ago!

3 c. rice chex cereal

3 c. wheat chex cereal

3 c. corn chex cereal

1½ c. mixed nuts

1 c. pretzel sticks

6 tbsp. butter

2 tbsp. Worcestershire sauce

1½ tsp. seasoned salt

¾ tsp. onion salt

½ tsp. garlic salt

Preheat the oven to 250 degrees Fahrenheit.

In a small bowl, microwave the butter to melt, about forty-five seconds. Stir in the Worcestershire sauce and remaining seasonings. In a large roasting pan, place all the dry ingredients. Pour butter mixture evenly over the dry ingredients, stirring to coat. Bake for one hour, stirring thoroughly every fifteen minutes. Spread on paper towels to cool. Store in an airtight container.

Speed Tip: In a hurry? Alternatively, you can place all the ingredients in a large microwavable bowl and microwave for six minutes, stirring every two minutes. Spread on paper towels to cool. Store in an airtight container.

264

Crackers and Dips

Dips might be the easiest of all party tray elements. Many don't require more than stirring a few ingredients together. You can serve them with chips, crackers, pita, or cut vegetables. You'll find I've mentioned my favorite dippers with most of these recipes. Adding your own homemade cheese straws or upgrading some store-bought crackers makes any party dip more special!

Cheese Straws

8 oz. grated extra-sharp cheddar cheese

1½ c. flour, plus more for dusting

1 tsp. salt

1 tsp. crushed red pepper flakes

1½ tbsp. roughly-chopped fresh herbs, such as rosemary or thyme

1 stick cold, unsalted butter

6 tbsp. heavy cream

Preheat the oven to 400 degrees Fahrenheit.

Line two baking sheets with parchment paper. Set aside. In a food processor, mix the cheese, flour, salt, pepper flakes, and herbs. Pulse until the mixture looks like coarse crumbs. Cut butter into small chunks and add into mixture. Pulse until the mixture is the size of small peas. Add the heavy cream and pulse until the mixture begins to form a dough. Lightly flour a work surface and place the dough on it, also flouring the top surface of the dough. With your hands, press dough into a rectangle about one inch thick. Divide dough into two pieces and roll out each half into an 8x10" rectangle pan about one eight-inch thick. Trim the dough using a sharp knife or pizza wheel, not wasting much on the edges. Cut into strips about one fourth-inch wide. Place onto baking pans with about one fourth-inch between. Bake for 10-12 minutes, turning baking sheets halfway through cooking. Remove from the oven and place on a wire rack to cool.

Crack Crackers

Remember that addictive Cracker Crack toffee I taught you to make? These crackers are equally easy and just as addictive on your appetizer tray.

⅓ c. olive oil

One 1 oz. package ranch dressing mix

1 tbsp. dried dill

1 tbsp. garlic powder

Two 16 oz. packages bite-size cheddar cheese crackers

Preheat the oven to 300 degrees Fahrenheit.

Mix together the olive oil, ranch dressing mix, dill, and garlic powder in a small bowl. In a large bowl, drizzle over crackers and toss to coat. Divide the crackers between two baking sheets and spread into an even layer on each. Bake for thirty minutes, stirring every ten minutes. Cool on baking sheets and store in an airtight tin or resealable plastic bag.

White Bean Hummus

Two 15.8 oz. cans Northern beans, drained

4 tbsp. olive oil

8 tbsp. fresh lemon juice

2 tsp. lemon zest

2 large cloves garlic

1 tbsp. fresh basil leaves

1 tbsp. fresh rosemary leaves

1 tbsp. fresh chives

½ tsp. salt

¼ tsp. freshly-ground pepper

Wash and dry the herbs. Roughly chop the basil. Place all ingredients except the herbs into a food processor. Pulse until combined. Add the herbs and continue to process until creamy and thick, but still with a little texture.

Spinach Dip

One 10 oz. package frozen spinach

1 c. sour cream

¾ c. mayonnaise

1 garlic clove, grated

2 scallions, thinly-sliced

One 8 oz. jar water chestnuts, drained and chopped

1 4 oz. jar pimentos, drained

½ tsp. Worcestershire sauce

½ tsp. salt

½ tsp. freshly-ground black pepper

1 loaf sourdough bread (not sliced) cut into 1-inch chunks

Pita chips, for serving

Assorted raw vegetables, for serving

Cook spinach according to package directions. Drain into a colander and then rinse with cold water. Place the spinach into the center of a clean kitchen towel and wring it out into the sink, removing as much water as possible. Chop spinach finely. Combine the spinach with the sour cream, mayonnaise, garlic, scallions, water chestnuts, pimentos, Worcestershire sauce, salt, and pepper, mixing well. Transfer to serving bowl and serve with sourdough bread, vegetables, and pita chips.

Guacamole

3 medium ripe avocados

⅓ c. grape tomatoes, chopped

2 tbsp. red onion, diced

2 tbsp. chopped cilantro

Juice of half a lime, divided

½ tsp. salt

1 small garlic clove, grated

Splash Worcestershire sauce

In a medium bowl, mash avocados to a chunky consistency. Add the tomatoes, onion, cilantro, half the lime juice, salt, garlic, and Worcestershire sauce, stirring to combine. Cover the surface with remaining lime juice. Cover the surface with plastic wrap, pressing into the top of the guacamole until there are no air bubbles. Refrigerate for up to two days.

Helpful Hint: Another way to keep guacamole from browning is to place the avocado pit into the bowl. Just be sure to remove it before serving!

Pimento Cheese

This is the classic Southern cheese spread. You can serve it on a dip tray, put dollops on top of crackers as appetizers, or make sandwiches with it.

One 4 oz. jar diced pimento, drained

1½ c. mayonnaise, preferably Duke's

¼ tsp. cayenne powder

One 8 oz. block extra-sharp cheddar cheese, finely-grated

One 8 oz. block sharp cheddar cheese, finely-grated

½ tsp. Worcestershire sauce

In a medium bowl, stir together pimento, mayonnaise, cayenne, and Worcestershire sauce. Add cheeses and blend well. Store in an airtight container in the refrigerator for up to one week.

Ro-Tel Dip

2 lb. Velveeta cheese, cubed

Two 10 oz. cans Ro-Tel tomatoes, medium or hot

One 8 oz. brick cream cheese

Two 15 oz. cans Hormel chili, no beans

Place all ingredients in a six-quart slow cooker set on high, stirring occasionally, until cheese is melted. Lower heat to low and keep warm, stirring occasionally, to prevent skin from forming on the surface. Serve with tortilla scoops.

Greek Yogurt Ranch Dip

1 c. plain Greek yogurt

¾ tsp. garlic powder

½ tsp. onion powder

½ tsp. dried dill

¼ tsp. salt

¼ tsp. Worcestershire sauce

⅛ tsp. cayenne pepper

Combine all ingredients in a small bowl. Cover with plastic wrap and chill until serving time. Serve with a variety of vegetables for dipping.

French Onion Dip

1 c. sour cream or Greek yogurt

1 tbsp. dried chopped onion

1 tsp. onion powder

1 pinch garlic powder

¼ tsp. salt

1 tbsp. chopped fresh parsley or 1 tsp. dried parsley

1 envelope french onion soup powder

Mix all ingredients until well-combined. Taste to check for salt level. Cover with plastic wrap and refrigerate until serving. Serve with salty potato chips or assorted vegetables.

Buffalo Chicken Dip

One 8 oz. package cream cheese, softened

1 c. hot sauce

1 c. ranch salad dressing

Three 4½ oz. cans chunk white chicken, drained and shredded

1 c. shredded cheddar cheese

Green onions, chopped (if desired)

Tortilla chips for serving

Celery sticks for serving

Preheat the oven to 350 degrees Fahrenheit.

In a medium bowl, mix cream cheese, hot sauce, and ranch dressing. Stir in chicken. Spread in the bottom of an 11x7" ungreased baking pan. Sprinkle cheese over top. Bake for 20-22 minutes until heated through. Serve with chips and celery.

Coconut Macaroon Fruit Dip

This will change your life! It's ridiculously good. You might gain fifty pounds, but even if you don't really like fruit (and I don't!), you'll love eating fruit with this dip.

1 package soft coconut macaroons, such as Archway

2 c. sour cream

¼ c. packed brown sugar

Crumble macaroons in a medium bowl. Stir in sour cream and brown sugar. Refrigerate overnight. Serve with assorted fruit. This is especially good served with firm, tart apples (like Granny Smith), and pears. Bananas are also great. Bananas and coconut are a natural combination.

Helpful Tips

Cooking is therapeutic when you do it thoughtfully and deliberately. Cooking will become a comfortable and comforting activity when you have the right tools and develop habits that make the job go smoothly. Since I can't be in your kitchen with you, here are some of the tips I give to everyone I teach.

Equipment Tips

The most important and versatile kitchen tool is a very sharp knife.

Invest in a cast iron skillet that is pre-seasoned.

Use a straw to cap (hull) strawberries, insert through the bottom of the berry and push up.

A vegetable peeler is good for slicing vegetables very thinly. It is also great for making curls of Parmesan cheese and even chocolate.

A mandoline can be indispensable. Always work slowly and use the guard to prevent cutting fingers.

Getting Started

Read the recipe before beginning preparation. Read it again.

Gather all foodstuffs and tools needed for the recipe together, so they are readily accessible.

Prepping Fruits and Vegetables

When prepping, always have a waste bowl to save you from making many trips to the trash can.

To peel garlic, smash with the side of a kitchen knife. The peel comes right off.

Chopping garlic is easier if you add a pinch of salt for abrasion.

Don't wash fresh mushrooms. Simply brush off any soil with a dry paper towel.

To slice a quantity of cherry tomatoes, place onto a plate, cover with a second plate and run your sharp knife in-between.

290

To chop an onion without tears, leave the root on, halve the onion, then chop.

To peel tomatoes more easily, cut an "X" on the bottom, and submerge in boiling water for 15-30 seconds. The same works for peaches.

Before juicing lemons or limes, place in the microwave for 7-10 seconds. Then, roll on the counter with your palm pressing firmly. They will yield twice as much juice.

For crispy fries or chips, cut potato into desired shapes, and soak in cold water for an hour. Pat dry before frying.

If fruit is not ripe, store in a paper bag with a banana. The banana emits a gas that ripens the other fruit faster.

Remove some heat from chilies by removing seeds and ribs.

Preparing Meats

Use two skewers when roasting or grilling to make food more manageable.

Let steak come to room temperature before seasoning and grilling.

When browning meat, work in batches. Never crowd the pan, that will steam the meat instead of crisping it.

About Eggs

Don't salt beaten eggs before cooking. It changes their texture. Save seasoning for the last minute.

Make an egg wash using one egg, whisked with one tablespoon of water. It acts as glue to stick pastry together and is then brushed over the surface of the dough to leave a shine.

For no-fail hard boiled-eggs, cover with water and bring to a boil. Turn off the heat, cover the pan, and allow to sit for twelve minutes. Gently "jostle" hard boiled-eggs against the side of the pan to break shells up, then peel under running water.

How to test eggs for freshness. Place in a glass of water. If the egg sinks and lays on its side, it is very fresh. If it sinks and stands on its end, it is a few weeks old. If it floats, it is not fresh.

Frying and Sautéing

When frying or sautéing,, warm the pan, add the oil, and warm it to a shimmer before adding food.

Butter has a much lower burn temperature than oil. Try using butter and oil in a 1:1 ratio to up the burning temperature so you can fry hotter.

Taste Testing

Always taste the food before adding more seasoning. That said, don't be afraid of salt, it enhances flavors.

Always give a dish a final taste before serving.

Cleaning Up

Handwash cutting boards with vinegar to get rid of bacteria.

Never wash cast iron. Sprinkle with kosher salt and scrub with a paper towel. Then spread a thin layer of oil over the surface and store.

Clean dishes as you go. That way, when it's time to sit down, you won't be dreading a mountain of dishes waiting for you, and you can enjoy friends and family.

Leftovers (and On-Purpose Leftovers!)

Make stock in large batches and freeze leftovers in resealable zipper bags.

Freeze leftover tomato paste, wine, and herbs in ice trays. To store the herbs, chop finely, and cover with water or olive oil.

Keeping Food Fresh

Wrap leafy greens in a damp paper towel and store in a resealable bag in the refrigerator. They will last much longer.

Place herbs in a small glass of water in the refrigerator to prolong freshness.

Keep guacamole from browning by leaving the pit in the bowl until serving time. You can also cover with lime or lemon juice and place plastic wrap over top, pressing down on the surface to prevent air bubbles.

When taking salad to a gathering, prevent it from being soggy by not dressing it until you arrive.

Celery will last a couple of months if you wrap it in aluminum foil before storing it in the refrigerator.

Food Rescue Tips (Throw Away Less!)

Never throw out vanilla pods. Submerge them in sugar for four weeks to make an infused sugar.

To soften hard brown sugar, add a slice of bread to the bag, and leave overnight.

Your cookies will stay soft if you store them with a slice of bread or apple. The bread and apple will become hard, but the cookies will stay soft and chewy.

New Uses for Your Kitchen Towels

When using a hand mixer, place a folded, damp kitchen towel under the bowl to stop it from slipping around on the countertop.

Place a damp towel under a cutting board to prevent it from sliding around.

Stubborn jar lid? Place a folded kitchen towel on the countertop, turn the jar upside down, and rap the lid sharply on the towel-covered counter. (Strike the lid straight up and down versus rapping along the side of the lid.) It should loosen right up.

Easy Substitutions

Don't have buttermilk? No worries! Add one tablespoon of vinegar or lemon juice to a measuring cup, then add milk to make a cup. Let sit for ten minutes before using.

You can make your own vanilla extract. Cut vanilla beans in half and submerge 3-5 beans in a pint of plain vodka. Store in a cool dark place for 6-12 months. Makes a great gift!

Last Tips

A pinch of salt in coffee grounds will reduce the bitterness.

The ratio for a vinaigrette is three parts oil to one part acid.

When serving ice cream to a large group, open the entire container and slice. This is much faster than trying to scoop portions.

How to Stretch Dinner for Unexpected Guests?

When you've learned to enjoy cooking these easy dishes, you'll discover that your unfussy but delicious meals make your home a magnet for unexpected guests. How do you stretch the meal you planned for four to serve six or eight?

 If your main for the evening is a soup, one way to extend it is to add some water, plus a parmesan rind. The parmesan will enrich the broth with flavor and a bit of thickening.

 Adding sides is the easiest strategy overall. Say you started with a meatloaf, expecting to serve four people two slices each. Now there are twice as many coming for dinner! Add a bread or a salad. Maybe take a couple twelve-ounce bags of vegetables out of the freezer and steam them for a side dish of peas or broccoli. Make some quick mashed potatoes.

 Sides are not just filling but they'll distract guests from wanting more servings of the main dish. You can always add more sides!

How to Enhance a Boxed Cake Mix?

Face it, there will be a time when you want cake or need one to take to a function, but don't have time to make it from scratch. Box cake mixes often leave a lot to be desired. You can fix that with just a few enhancements!

 When a mix asks for water, try buttermilk! The tangy buttermilk adds an element of richness and enhances the flavor of the cake.

 Add an extra egg. The egg works as a binder, holding everything together.

 Try melted butter instead of oil.

 Add spices or extracts to the mix. For example, when I make lemon pound cake, I add a teaspoon of lemon extract to make it extra lemony. People can't believe it came from a box!

 When I am using a box cake, I buy a corresponding flavor of pudding mix. Don't prepare the pudding, just add it dry right to the cake mix. It changes everything!

 When making chocolate cake, a teaspoon of espresso powder is a total game-changer.

 The same goes for homemade frostings. Vanilla extract enhances the flavor in vanilla frosting. Espresso powder works well with chocolate buttercream frosting. Lemon extract enhances tartness in lemon frostings. Experiment until you find the one that makes you swoon.

Abbreviations

- **Teaspoon** - tsp.
- **Tablespoon** - tbsp.
- **Cup** - c.
- **Pint** - pt.
- **Quart** - qt.

- **Gallon** - gal.
- **Ounce** - oz.
- **Fluid ounce** - fl. oz.
- **Pound** - lb.

Converting Measurements

Liquid measurements

- **2 tbsp.** = 1 oz. = ⅛ cup
- **16 tbsp.** = 8 oz. = 1 cup = ½ pint = ¼ quart
- **32 tbsp.** = 16 oz. = 2 cups = 1 pint = ½ quart = ⅛ gallon

- **64 tbsp.** = 32 oz. = 4 cups = 2 pints = 1 quart = ¼ gallon
- **256 tbsp.** = 128 oz. = 16 cups = 8 pints = 4 quarts = 1 gallon

Dry measurements

- **3 tsp.** = 1 tbsp.
- **12 tsp.** = 4 tbsp. = ¼ cup

- **16 tsp.** = 5 tbsp. + 1 tsp. = ⅓ cup
- **24 tsp.** = 8 tbsp. = ½ cup

An Alphabetical Glossary of Cooking Terms

No matter how long you cook, you'll find yourself learning new terms as you learn new techniques. These are terms you'll find in the kind of easy recipes in this cookbook for those just beginning to expand their cooking skills. You can use this section as a reference to terms you find in this cookbook.

- **AU GRATIN**

  Sprinkled with breadcrumbs and cheese, or both, and browned. The phrase 'au gratin' literally means "by grating" in French, or "with a crust."

- **AU JUS**

  With its own juices from cooking, often refers to steak or other meat.

- **BASTE**

  To pour melted fat, pan juices, or other liquid over meat or other food while cooking to keep it moist.

- **BLANCH**

  A quick method of cooking food, usually green vegetables, so they remain a bright green and hold their firmness. The food is briefly scalded in boiling hot water, then plunged into ice cold water.

- **BROIL**

  Ovens have a setting for broiling, which

  To broil is to cook with high temperature heat from the top only. The broil setting on your oven turns on just the upper heating element. Food is placed on an oven tray under the preheated element.

- **BRAISE**

  Braising combines dry and moist heat, and is helpful in preparing tougher cuts of meat. The meat is seared at high heat (dry), then slowly cooked in liquid (moist).

- **BRINING**

  The process of soaking meat in a brine (heavily-salted water) before cooking. This has become popular in preparing holiday turkeys.

- **BLEND**

  Combining two or more ingredients to a smooth, uniform texture.

- **BONE**

  One of those odd terms. To bone a piece of meat is to remove its bones.

- **CLARIFY**

  Usually refers to butter. By gently melting the butter, the milk solids and water separate from the butterfat. The solids are then skimmed.

- **CORING**

  Removing seeds and other tough material from the center of a fruit.

- **CURDLE**

  When egg-based mixtures are cooked too fast, the protein separates from the liquids, leaving a lumpy mixture behind. When dairy products are inadequately refrigerated, they likewise curdle, although this can be useful for making a soft cheese.

- **CUT IN**

  A way of blending fats with flour. The method often refers to using a pastry blender or knives to mix butter or shortening into flour until the mixture clumps to a specified size, usually peas or cornmeal.

- **DICE**

  To cut with a knife into a small cube. The size may vary.

- **DOLLOP**

  A serving size and a casual cooking measure. When a recipe calls for a "dollop" of something, the amount doesn't need to be precise. Yogurt, whipped cream, and mashed potatoes are among the foods that might be dolloped as garnishes, servings, or ingredients.

- **DREDGING**

  To coat moist foods with a dry ingredient before cooking.

- **DRESS**

  Dress has two definitions when it comes to cooking. Most often it means to coat foods (generally salads) in a sauce. It also refers to preparing meats and fish for cooking, by sectioning the meat from the carcass.

- **DEEP FRY**

  To cook food in a deep layer of hot oil.

- **DEGLAZE**

  To loosen bits of food that have stuck on the bottom of a pan by adding liquid such as stock or wine.

- **FILET**

  Most commonly used for a very tender cut of beef, but can also refer to the meat of chicken and fish.

- **FLAKE**

  Refers to the process of gently breaking off small pieces of food, often for combining with other foods. For example, you would flake cooked fish to combine with cooked, mashed potatoes, to make fish cakes.

- **GRILL**

  Grilling food is applying dry heat to food either from above or below. In some countries, grilling refers to cooking food under the grill in your oven (in the States this is called broiling) or can also refer to cooking food in a pan with grill lines. In the States, grilling is often done on an outdoor cooker.

- **GLAZE**

  A glaze is a sticky substance coating a food. It is usually referenced in baking, but also in relation to cooking meats, where a marinade will be brushed over the food continuously to form a glaze.

- **GRATIN**

  A gratin is a topping that is often either breadcrumbs or grated cheese that forms a brown crust when placed under a hot grill.

- **GREASE**

  Refers to applying a fat to a roasting tray or cake tin to ensure that food doesn't stick.

- **GRIND**

  To break something down into much smaller pieces, for example, coffee beans or whole spices, using some kind of grinding tool, which could be a mortar and pestle or a coffee-style grinder.

- **HULL**

  A hull is the husk, shell, or external covering of a fruit, nut, or grain. More specifically, it is the leafy green part of a strawberry. To hull (verb) is to remove a hull.

- **INFUSE**

  You infuse a food with the flavor of another ingredient when, for instance, you put a vanilla bean or orange zest in hot milk to flavor a pudding. Sugars may also be infused with flavors. See also "Steep."

- **JULIENNE**

  Refers to a knife cut that produces thin shapes like matchsticks.

- **KNEAD**

  To work dough into a soft, uniform, and malleable texture by pressing, folding, and stretching with the heel of your hand.

- **MACERATE**

  To soak an ingredient, usually fruit, in a liquid so that it takes on the flavor of the liquid. Cut fresh fruits are sometimes macerated with sugar alone, which draws out liquid from the fruit to create the macerating liquid. This technique can also be used to soften dried fruit

- **MARINATE**

  When you marinate meat or vegetables, the flavors of the marinade get into it and improve the dish. Some marinades also help to tenderize meats.

- **MINCE**

  To cut food into small uniform pieces: smaller than diced or chopped foods.

- **MISE EN PLACE**

  This French phrase, pronounced MEEZ ohn PLAS, means to put things in their place. In cooking, it refers to preparing ingredients—such as dicing onions, chopping veggies, or measuring spices—before starting to cook.

- **PAR COOK**

  Cooking food so it is only partially done, and can be finished or reheated later.

- **PARBOIL**

  A brief boil, often used to soften foods like potatoes before roasting or grilling them, so as to speed up the cooking process.

- **POACH**

  To cook in gently bubbling liquids such as a stock, broth, or wine-based syrup. Fish, some fruits, and eggs are often poached.

- **PURÉE**

  Mashing or blending cooked food, usually vegetables, to a paste-like consistency.

- **PICKLE**

  Preserving food in a salt or vinegar brine.

- **REDUCE**

  Simmering or boiling a liquid, usually a stock or a sauce, to thicken it or intensify the flavor.

- **RENDER**

  Using a low heat to melt the fat away from a food item, usually a piece of meat. This rendered fat can then be used for cooking.

- **ROAST**

  A method of dry cooking a piece of meat, where hot air around the food allows it to cook evenly and brown nicely.

- **ROUX**

  A roux (pronounced ROO) is a flour and fat mixture cooked together, which acts as a thickener in soups, stews, and sauces.

- **RECONSTITUTE**

  To restore a dried food to its original consistency, or to change its texture, by letting it soak in warm water.

- **REFRESH**

  To halt the cooking process, usually that of vegetables after being blanched, by plunging them into ice-cold water.

- **SAUTÉ**

  Saute (SAW-tay) means "to jump" in French. Sauteeing is cooking food in a minimal amount of oil over a rather high heat.

- **SCALD**

  To heat a liquid so it's right about to reach the boiling point, where small bubbles start to appear around the edges.

- **SCORE**

  To score is to make shallow, diagonal cuts on the surface of meat, vegetables, and some breads. It helps to render fat, make the food more crisp, and absorb flavors from (for example) a glaze.

- **SEAR OR BROWN**

  A method of cooking food over a high heat until the surface browns or caramelizes. This is often done before braising a food, to give it added flavor. It is not usually intended to cook the food all the way through.

- **SHALLOW FRY**

  To cook food in a shallow layer of preheated oil.

- **SIMMER**

  Process of cooking in hot liquids that are kept just below the boiling point.

- **SKIM**

  To remove a top layer of fat or scum that has developed on the surface of soups, stocks, or sauces.

- **STEAM**

  Cooking food by using steam.

- **STEEP**

  Steeping is the process of allowing dried ingredients to soak in a liquid until the liquid has taken on the flavor of the ingredient.

- **SWEAT**

  This refers to the gentle cooking of vegetables in butter or oil under a lid, so that their natural liquid is released to aid the cooking process. Often vegetables cooked this way will end up looking translucent.

- **TEMPER**

  To temper is the process of adding a small quantity of a hot liquid to a cold liquid in order to warm the cold liquid slightly. This is often done before adding delicate ingredients like eggs to a hot mixture. To prevent the eggs from curdling or scrambling, you slowly add a little of the hot mix to the eggs, stirring all the while, before adding the warmed eggs into the hot mixture. Another example would be how you add a cornstarch slurry to a hot mixture. A little of the hot mixture is added to the slurry before adding the slurry into the main hot mixture. This prevents cornstarch lumps in your sauce.

- **TRUSS**

  To bind the legs and wings of a bird to its body, ensuring it maintains an even shape so that none of the extremities dry out while roasting.

- **WHIP**

  The process of beating food with a whisk to incorporate air and to increase volume.

- **WHISK**

  The process of using a whisk to blend ingredients together smoothly or to incorporate air into food.

- **ZEST**

  Removing the outer part of citrus peel (called the zest) either by using a grater, a peeler, or a knife.

Just that I have seen **Samaritan's Purse** arrived first in disasters and I am proud to partner with them in their efforts around the world. I happened to be a travel nurse in Paducah, when a neighboring town was completely destroyed by a tornado. They were there the very next day. I admire their efforts and they will go anywhere to **help, heal, and spread the good news of Jesus**.

https://www.samaritanspurse.org/